I0014803

Arduino Interesting projects like 3D Printing and piano tones using circuits

Copyright © Anbazhagan.k
All rights reserved 2019.

Arduino Interesting projects like 3D Printing and piano tones using circuits

CONTENTS

CONTENTS

ACKNOWLEDGMENTS

The writer might want to recognize the diligent work of the article group in assembling this book. He might likewise want to recognize the diligent work of the Raspberry Pi Foundation and the Arduino bunch for assembling items and networks that help to make the Internet Of Things increasingly open to the overall population. Yahoo for the democratization of innovation!

INTRODUCTION

The Internet of Things (IOT) is a perplexing idea comprised of numerous PCs and numerous correspondence ways. Some IOT gadgets are associated with the Internet and some are most certainly not. Some IOT gadgets structure swarms that convey among themselves. Some are intended for a solitary reason, while some are increasingly universally useful PCs. This book is intended to demonstrate to you the IOT from the back to front. By structure IOT gadgets, the per user will comprehend the essential ideas and will almost certainly develop utilizing the rudiments to make his or her very own IOT applications. These included ventures will tell the per user the best way to assemble their very own IOT ventures and to develop the models appeared. The significance of Computer Security in IOT gadgets is additionally talked about and different systems for protecting the IOT from unapproved clients or programmers. The most significant takeaway from this book is in structure the tasks yourself.

1.AUTOMATIC WATER DISPENSER USING ARDUINO

About 71% of earth is secured with water, yet tragic-ally just 2.5% of it is drinking water. With ascend in populace, contamination and environmental change, it is normal that by when 2025 we will encounter enduring water deficiencies. At one hand there are as of now minor questions among countries and states for sharing waterway water then again we as people squander a great deal of drinking water because of our carelessness.

It probably won't show up enormous at the first run through, yet in the event that your tap dribbled a drop of water once consistently it would take just around five hours for you to squander one gallon of water, that is sufficient water for a normal human to get by for two days. So what should be possible to stop this? As consistently the appropriate response, for this, lies with progress in innovation. In case we supplant all the manual taps with a keen one that opens and closes without anyone else naturally we can spare water as well as have a more beneficial way of life since we don't need to work the tap with our grimy hands. So in this undertaking we will assemble an Automatic Water Dispenser utilizing Arduino as well as a Solenoid valve that can naturally give you water when a glass is put close to it. Sounds cool right! So how about we construct one...

Materials Required

- Arduino Uno (any version)
- Solenoid Valve
- IRF540 MOSFET
- HCSR04 - Ultrasonic Sensor
- Breadboard
- 1k as well as 10k Resistor
- Connecting Wires

Working Concept

The Concept behind the Automatic Water Dispenser is basic. We will utilize a HCSRO4 Ultrasonic Sensor to check if any item with the end goal that the glass is put before the container. A solenoid valve will be utilized to control the progression of water, which is when empowered the water will stream out and when de-invigorated the water will be halted. So we will compose an Arduino program which consistently checks in the event that any item is put close to the tap, in the event that indeed, at that point the solenoid will be turned on and hold up till the article is expelled, when the item is evacuated the solenoid will mood killer naturally in this way shutting the inventory of water. Get familiar with utilizing Ultrasonic sensor with Arduino here.

Circuit Diagram

The total circuit graph for Arduino based water Dispenser is demonstrated as follows

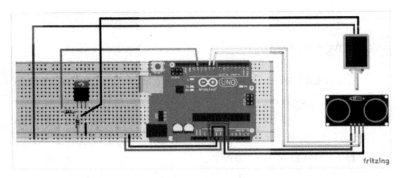

The solenoid valve utilized in this venture is a 12V valve with a most extreme current rating of 1.2A and a nonstop current rating of 700mA. That is the point at which the Valve is turned on it will devour about 700mA to keep the valve turned on. As we probably am aware an Arduino is a Development board which works with 5V and consequently we need an exchanging driver circuit for the Solenoid to turn it on and off.

The exchanging gadget utilized in this task is the IRF540N N-Channel MOSFET. It has the 3 pins Gate, Source and Drain from stick 1 individually. As appeared in the circuit graph the positive terminal of the solenoid is fueled with the Vin stick of the Arduino. Since we will utilize a 12V connector to control the Arduino and along these lines the Vin stick will yield 12V which can be utilized to control the Solenoid. The -ve terminal of the solenoid is associated with the ground through the MOSFET's Source and Drain pins. So the solenoid will be fueled just if the MOSFET is turned on.

The door stick of the MOSFET is utilized to turn it on or off. It will stay off if the door stick is grounded and will turn on if an entryway voltage is connected. To keep the MOSFET killed when no voltage is connected to door stick, the entryway stick is destroyed to ground however a 10k resistor. The Arduino stick 12 is utilized to kill on or the MOSFET, so the D12 stick is associated with the door stick through a 1K resistor. This 1K resistor is utilized for current restricting reason.

The Ultrasonic Sensor is fueled by the +5V as well as ground pins of the Arduino. The Echo and Trigger stick is associated with the stick 8 and stick 9 separately. We would then be able to program the Arduino to utilize the Ultrasonic sensor to gauge the separation and turn on the MOSFET when an item is identify. The entire circuit is basic and henceforth can be effectively expand over a breadboard. Mine looked something like this beneath subsequent to making the associations.

Programming the Arduino Board

For this venture we need to compose a program which uses the HCSR-04 Ultrasonic sensor to gauge the separation of the item before it. At the point when the separation is under 10cm we need to turn on the MOSFET and else we need to mood killer the MOSFET. We will likewise utilize the on board LED associated with stick 13 and switch it alongside the MOSFET so we can guarantee if the MOSFET is in turned on or off state. The total program to do the equivalent is given toward the part of the bargain. Just underneath I have clarified the program by breaking it into little important scraps.

The program begins with macros definition. We have the trigger and reverberation stick for the Ultrasonic sensor and the MOSFET entryway stick and LED as the I/O for our Arduino. So we have characterized to which stick these will be associated with. In our equipment we have associated the Echo and Trigger stick to 8 and ninth computerized stick separately. At that point the MOSFET stick is associated with stick 12 and the locally available LED as a matter of course is associated with stick 13. We characterize a similar utilizing the accompanying lines

```
#define trigger 9

#define echo 8

#define LED 13

#define MOSFET 12
```

Inside the arrangement work we proclaim which pins are information and which are yield. In our equipment just the Echo stick of Ultrasonic(US) sensor is the information stick and rest all are yield pins. So we utilize the pinMode capacity of Arduino to indicate equivalent to demonstrated as follows

```
pinMode(trigger,OUTPUT);

pinMode(echo,INPUT);

pinMode(LED,OUTPUT);

pinMode(MOSFET,OUTPUT);
```

Inside the principle circle work we require the capacity called measure_distance(). This capacity utilizes the US sensor to gauge the separation of the article before it and updates the incentive to the variable 'separation'. To quantify separation utilizing US sensor the trigger stick should initially be held low for two miniaturized scale seconds and afterward held high for ten microseconds and again held low for two small scale seconds. This will send a sonic impact of Ultrasonic sign into the air which will get reflected by the article before it and the reverberation stick will get the sign reflected by it. At that point we utilize the time taken an incentive to compute separation of the item in front of the sensor. In the event that you need to know more on the best way to interface HC-SR04 Ultrasonic sensor with Arduino, read however the connection. The program to ascertain the separation is give beneath

```
digitalWrite(trigger,LOW);

delayMicroseconds(2);

digitalWrite(trigger,HIGH);

delayMicroseconds(10);

digitalWrite(trigger,LOW);
```

```
delayMicroseconds(2);

time=pulseIn(echo,HIGH);

distance=time*340/20000;
```

When the separation is determined, we need to analyze the estimation of separation utilizing a basic if articulation and if the worth is under 10cm we make the MOSFET and LED to go high, in the accompanying else proclamation we make the MOSFET and LED to go low. The program to do the equivalent is demonstrated as follows.

```
if(distance<10)

{

    digitalWrite(LED,HIGH);digitalWrite(MOS-
FET,HIGH);

}

else

{

    digitalWrite(LED,LOW);digitalWrite(MOS-
FET,LOW);
```

}

Working of Automatic Water Dispenser

Make the associations as appeared in the circuit and transfer the beneath given program into your Arduino board. Make some basic game plan to interface the solenoid valve to the water delta and catalyst the circuit utilizing the 12V connector to the DC jack of Arduino board. Ensure the on board LED is killed, this guarantees the Solenoid is additionally off. The setup that I have made to exhibit the venture is demonstrated as follows

As should be obvious I have put the Ultrasonic sensor legitimately underneath the solenoid valve with the end goal that when the glass/tumbler is put beneath the solenoid it gets straightforwardly inverse to the ultrasonic sensor. This item will be detected by the

ultrasonic sensor and the MOSFET alongside the LED will turn ON accordingly making the solenoid to open and the water streams down.

Essentially when the glass is expelled the ultrasonic sensor advises to the Arduino there is no glass before it and therefore the Arduino shuts the valve.

Cautioning: Different Solenoid vales have diverse working voltage and current rating, ensure your solenoid works on 12V and expends not more than 1.5A greatest.

Code

```
#define trigger 9
#define echo 8
#define LED 13
#define MOSFET 12


float time=0,distance=0;


void setup()
{
Serial.begin(9600);
 pinMode(trigger,OUTPUT);
pinMode(echo,INPUT);
pinMode(LED,OUTPUT);
pinMode(MOSFET,OUTPUT);
```

```
 delay(2000);
}


void loop()
{
measure_distance();
 if(distance<10)
 {
        digitalWrite(LED,HIGH);digitalWrite(MOS-
FET,HIGH);
 }
 else
 {
        digitalWrite(LED,LOW);digitalWrite(MOS-
FET,LOW);
 }
 delay(500);
}
void measure_distance()
{
digitalWrite(trigger,LOW);
delayMicroseconds(2);
digitalWrite(trigger,HIGH);
delayMicroseconds(10);
digitalWrite(trigger,LOW);
delayMicroseconds(2);
time=pulseIn(echo,HIGH);


distance=time*340/20000;
```

```
}
```

2.RECORD AND PLAY 3D PRINTED ROBOTIC ARM

USING ARDUINO

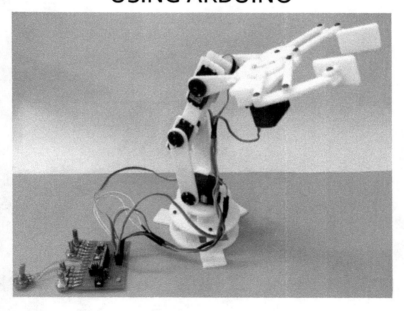

Automated Arms have substantiated themselves helpful and progressively gainful in numerous applications where speed, exactness and wellbeing is required. Yet, to me, what's more than that is these things are cool to take a gander at when they work. I have consistently wanted for an automated arm that could assist me with my day by day works simply like Dum-E and Dum-U that Tony obvious uses in his lab. These two bots can be seen helping him while building the Iron man suits or taping his work utilizing a camcorder. As a matter of fact Dum-E has likewise spared his life once....... furthermore, this is the place I might want to stop it since this is no fan Page. Aside from the anecdotal world there are many cool genuine Robotic Arms made by Fanuc, Kuka, Denso, ABB, Yaskawa and so forth. These automated arms are utilized in Production line of cars, mining plants, Chemical businesses and numerous different spots.

Along these lines, in this instructional exercise we are going to manufacture our very own Robotic Arm with the assistance of Arduino and MG995 Servo engines. The Robot will have a sum of 4 DOF barring the gripper and can be constrained by a potentiometer. Aside from that we will likewise program it to have a Record and play include with the goal that we can record a movement and request that the Robotic Arm rehash it the same number of times as we need it. Sounds cool right!!! So lets start building....

Material Required

- Arduino Nano
- 5-Potentiometer
- 5 MG-995 Servo Motor
- Servo horns

- Perf Board
- Nuts and Screws

Note: The body of the mechanical arm is totally 3D Printer. In case you have a printer you can print them utilizing the given structure documents. Else, utilizes the 3D model gave and machine your parts utilizing wood or acrylic. In case you don't have anything, at that point you can simply utilize cardboards to fabricate straightforward Robotic Arm.

3D Printing and Assembling the Robotic Arm

The most tedious part in structure this automated Arm is while building its body. At first I begun by planning the body utilizing Solidworks, yet later understood that there are numerous great structures promptly accessible on Thingiverse and there is no compelling reason to re-create the wheel. So I experienced the plans and found that the Robotic Arm V2.0 by Ashing will work superbly with our MG995 Servo Motors and would precisely suit our motivation.

So get to his Thingiverse page (connect given above) as well as install the model records. There are absolutely 14 sections which must be printed and the STL documents for every one of them can be downloaded from Thingiverse page. I utilized the Cura 3.2.1 Software from Ultimaker to cut the STL documents and my TEVO tarantula 3D printer to print them. On the off chance that you need to know more on 3D printer and how it functions you can peruse this article on

Beginners Guide to Getting Started with 3D Printing.

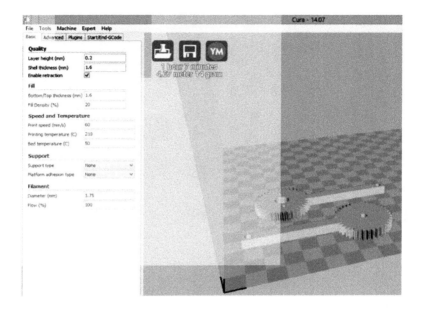

Fortunately none of the parts have over hanging structures so supports are not required. The Design is entirely plain and henceforth can be effectively dealt with by any essential 3D printer. Around after 4.5 long periods of printing every one of the parts are prepared to be gathered. The get together guidelines are again perfectly clarified by Ashing itself and henceforth I am not going to cover it.

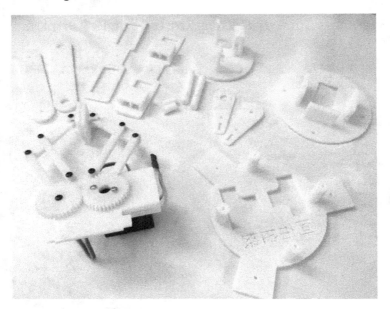

One little tip is that you would need to sand/document the edges of the parts for the engines to fit in. Every one of the engines will fit in vey cozy with a smidgen of mechanical power. Have tolerance and utilize a document to make space for the engines on the off chance that they appear to be somewhat tight. You would need like 20 quantities of 3mm jolts to gather the Robotic ARM.

When mounting an engine ensure it can turn and arrive at the ideal places before screwing it forever. Subsequent to collecting, you can continue with expanding the wires of the best three servo engines. I have utilized the male to female wires to extend them and carry it to circuit board. Ensure you outfit the wires appropriately with the goal that they don't come into your way while the Arm is working. Once amassed my mechanical Arm Looked something like this in the image underneath.

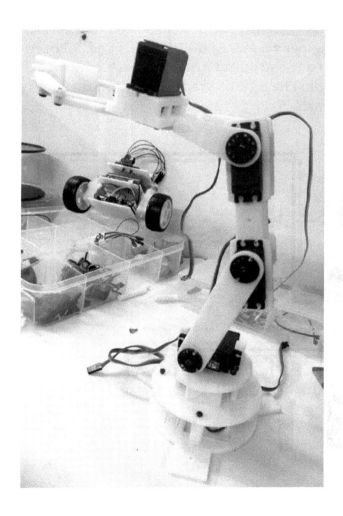

Circuit Diagram

The MG995 Servo engines work with 5V and the Arduino board has a 5V controller with it. So making the circuit is extremely simple. We need to interface 5 Servo engines to Arduino PWM pins and 5 Potentiometers to the Arduino Analog pins to control the Servo Motor. The circuit graph for the equivalent is given beneath.

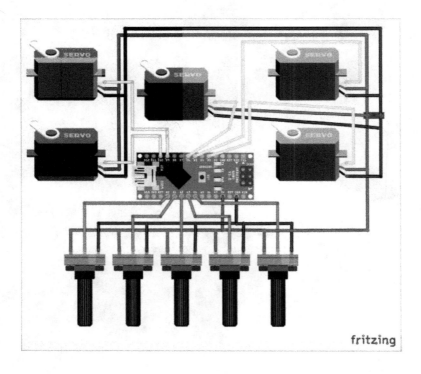

For this circuit I have not utilized any outside power

source. The Arduino is controlled through the USB port and the +5v stick on the board is utilized to control the potentiometer and the Servo engines. In our Robotic Arm at some random case of time just a single servo engine will be moving henceforth the current devoured will be under 150mA which can be sourced by the on-board voltage controller of the Arduino Board.

We have 5 Servo engine and 5 potentiometers to control them individually. These 5 potentiometers are associated with the 5 Analog pins A0 to A4 of the Arduino board. The Servo engines are constrained by PWM flag so we need to associate them to the PWM pins of Arduino. On Arduino Nano the pins D3,D5,D6,D9 and D11 just underpins PWM, so we utilize the initial 5 pins for our servo engines. I have utilized a perf board to weld the associations and my board looked something like this underneath when finished. I have additionally added a barrel jack to control the gadget through battery whenever required. Anyway it is totally discretionary.

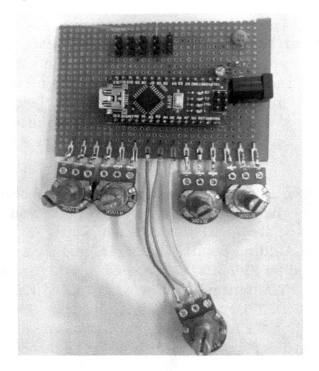

In the event that you are totally new with Servo engines and Arduino, at that point you are prescribed to peruse the Basics of Servo engine and Controlling Servo with Arduino article before you continue with the venture.

Programming Arduino for Robotic Arm

Presently, the fun part is to program the Arduino to enable the client to record the developments made utilizing the POT and afterward play it when required. To do this we need to program the Arduino for 2 modes. One is the Record mode, other is the Play mode. The client can flip between the two modes by utilizing the sequential screen. The total program to do the equivalent can be found at the base of this page, you can utilize the program for what it's worth. However, further underneath I have clarified the program with little scraps for you to get it.

As consistently we start the program by including the required header records. Here the Servo.h header record is utilized to control the servo engines. We have 5 Servo engines and consequently 5 items are pronounced giving each engine a name. We likewise initialise the factors that we will use in the progam. I have proclaimed them all as worldwide yet you can change their extension on the off chance that you are keen on improving the program. We have additionally pronounced a cluster called saved_data which as the name states will spare all the recorded developments of the Robotic ARM.

#include <Servo.h> //Servo header file

//Declare object for 5 Servo Motors

Servo Servo_0;

Servo Servo_1;

Servo Servo_2;

```
Servo Servo_3;

Servo Gripper;

//Global Variable Declaration

int S0_pos, S1_pos, S2_pos, S3_pos, G_pos;

int  P_S0_pos,  P_S1_pos,  P_S2_pos,  P_S3_pos,
P_G_pos;

int  C_S0_pos,  C_S1_pos,  C_S2_pos,  C_S3_pos,
C_G_pos;

int POT_0,POT_1,POT_2,POT_3,POT_4;

int saved_data[700]; //Array for saving recorded
data

int array_index=0;

char incoming = 0;

int action_pos;

int action_servo;
```

Inside the void arrangement work we start the Serial correspondence at 9600 baud rate. We additionally indicate the stick to which the Servo engines are appended to. Here for our situation we have utilized the pins 3,5,6,9 and 10 which is determined utilizing the join work. Since the arrangement capacity keeps running during the beginning up we can utilize it to set our Robotic arm in a beginning position. So I have hardcoded the position an incentive for each of the five engines.

These hardcoded qualities can be changed by your inclination later. Toward the part of the arrangement we print a sequential line requesting that the client press R or P to do the comparing activity

```
void setup() {

Serial.begin(9600); //Serial Monitor for Debugging

//Decalre the pins to which the Servo Motors are connected to

Servo_0.attach(3);

Servo_1.attach(5);

Servo_2.attach(6);

Servo_3.attach(9);

Gripper.attach(10);
```

```
//Write the servo motors to intial position

Servo_0.write(70);

Servo_1.write(100);

Servo_2.write(110);

Servo_3.write(10);

Gripper.write(10);

Serial.println("Press 'R' to Record and 'P' to
play"); //Instrust the user

}
```

I have characterized a capacity called Read_POT which peruses the simple estimations of all the 5 potentiometers and maps it to the Servo position esteems. As we probably am aware the Arduino has a 8-piece ADC which gives us a yield from 0-1023 however the servo engines position esteems ranges from just 0-180. Likewise since these servo engines are not exceptionally exact it isn't protected to drive them to the extraordinary 0 end or 180 end so we set 10-170 as our points of confinement. We utilize the guide capacity to change over 0-1023 to 10-170 for all the five engine as demonstrated as follows.

```
void Read_POT() //Function to read the Analog
value form POT and map it to Servo value

{

  POT_0 = analogRead(A0); POT_1 = analo-
gRead(A1); POT_2 = analogRead(A2); POT_3 =
analogRead(A3); POT_4 = analogRead(A4); //Read
the Analog values form all five POT

  S0_pos = map(POT_0,0,1024,10,170); //Map it
for 1st Servo (Base motor)

  S1_pos = map(POT_1,0,1024,10,170); //Map it
for 2nd Servo (Hip motor)

  S2_pos = map(POT_2,0,1024,10,170); //Map it
for 3rd Servo (Shoulder motor)

  S3_pos = map(POT_3,0,1024,10,170); //Map it
for 4th Servo (Neck motor)

  G_pos = map(POT_4,0,1024,10,170); //Map it
for 5th Servo (Gripper motor)

}
```

Recording Mode Code

In the account mode the client needs to control the bot utilizing the Potentiometers. Each POT compares to an individual engine, as the pot is differed we should spare the situation of the engine and the engine number inside the saved_data cluster. We should perceive how that is accomplished utilizing the Record work.

Eliminating Jitter problem with Servo

When working with these Servo engines one normal issue that everybody may go over is that the engines may jitter while working. There are numerous answer for this issue, first you have sort out if the issue is with the control hardware of the Motor or with the estimation of position that is kept in touch with the servo engine. For my situation I utilized the sequential screen and found that the estimation of servo_pos isn't left steady and at some point nerves up/down haphazardly.

So I customized the Arduino to peruse the POT esteems twice and look at both the qualities. The worth will be taken as substantial just if both the qualities are same, else the worth will be disposed of. Fortunately this tackled the jitter issue for me. Additionally ensure that the POT is mounted solidly (I fastened it) to the Analog stick of the Arduino. Any lose association will likewise cause butterflies. The factors P_x_pos is utilized to spare the old qualities and afterward again the x_pos qualities are perused and mapped utilizing the above talked about Read_POT work.

Read_POT(); //Read the POT values for 1st time

//Save it in a varibale to compare it later

    P_S0_pos = S0_pos;

    P_S1_pos = S1_pos;

    P_S2_pos = S2_pos;

    P_S3_pos = S3_pos;

    P_G_pos = G_pos;

Read_POT(); //Read the POT value for 2nd time

Presently, we need to control the situation of the servo engine if the worth is legitimate. Likewise in the wake of controlling we need to spare the engine number and engine position in the exhibit. We could have utilized two distinctive exhibit one for engine number and the other for its position, however to spare memory and multifaceted nature I have consolidated them two by increasing the value of the pos esteem before sparing it in the cluster.

```
if (P_S0_pos == S0_pos) //If 1st and 2nd value are
same

{

    Servo_0.write(S0_pos); //Control the servo

    if (C_S0_pos != S0_pos) //If the POT has been
turned

    {

        saved_data[array_index] = S0_pos + 0; //Save
the new position to the array. Zero is added for
zeroth motor (for understading purpose)

        array_index++; //Increase the array index

    }

    C_S0_pos = S0_pos; //Saved the previous value
to check if the POT has been turned

}
```

The differentiator esteem for Sero_0 is 0 as well as
for Servo_1 is 1000 also for Servo_3 it is 3000 as well
as for Gripper it is 4000. The lines of code where the

differentiator is added to the estimation of position and spared to the exhibit is demonstrated as follows.

> **saved_data[array_index] = S0_pos + 0; //Save the new position to the array. Zero is a**
>
> **dded for zeroth motor (for understading purpose)**
>
> **saved_data[array_index] = S1_pos + 1000; //1000 is added for 1st servo motor as differentiater**
>
> **saved_data[array_index] = S2_pos + 2000; //2000 is added for 2nd servo motor as differentiater**
>
> **saved_data[array_index] = S3_pos + 3000; //3000 is added for 3rd servo motor as differentiater**
>
> **saved_data[array_index] = G_pos + 4000; //4000 is added for 4th servo motor as differentiater**

Playing mode Code

After the client has recorded the developments in the saved_data he can flip to the play mode by entering 'P" in the sequential screen. Inside the play mode we approach every component spared in the cluster and split the incentive to get the engine number and engine position and control their position appropriately.

Anbazhagan k

We utilize a for circle to explore through each component of the cluster the upto the qualities which are spared in the exhibit. At that point we utilize two factors action_servo and action_pos to get the quantity of servo engine to be controlled and its position individually. To get the quantity of servo engine we need to partition it by 1000 and to get the position we need the last three digits which can be acquired by taking a modulus.

For instance in case the worth spared in the exhibit is 3125, at that point it implies that the third engine must be moved to the situation of 125.

```
for (int Play_action=0; Play_action<array_index;
Play_action++) //Navigate through every saved
element in the array

{

    action_servo  =  saved_data[Play_action]  /
1000; //The fist charector of the array element is
split for knowing the servo number

    action_pos  =  saved_data[Play_action]  %
1000; //The last three charectors of the array
element is split to know the servo postion
```

Presently all that is left to do it utilize the servo number and move it to that acquired estimation of servo position. I have utilized a change case to get into the comparing servo engine number and the compose capacity to move the servo engine to that position. The switch case is demonstrated as follows

```
switch(action_servo){ //Check which servo motor should be controlled

    case 0: //If zeroth motor

      Servo_0.write(action_pos);

    break;

    case 1://If 1st motor

      Servo_1.write(action_pos);

    break;

    case 2://If 2nd motor

      Servo_2.write(action_pos);

    break;

    case 3://If 3rd motor
```

```
    Servo_3.write(action_pos);

  break;

  case 4://If 4th motor

    Gripper.write(action_pos);

  break;
```

Main *loop* function

Inside the fundamental circle work, we just need to check what the client has entered through the sequential screen and execute the record method of the play mode in like manner. The variable approaching is utilized to hold the estimation of the client. On the off chance that 'R' is entered Record mode will be enacted and if 'P' whenever squeezed Play mode will be executed by if contingent explanations as demonstrated as follows.

```
void loop() {

if (Serial.available() > 1) //If something is recevied
from serial monitor

{
```

```
incoming = Serial.read();

if (incoming == 'R')

Serial.println("Robotic          Arm          Recording
Started......");

if (incoming == 'P')

Serial.println("Playing Recorded sequence");

}

if (incoming == 'R') //If user has selected Record
mode

Record();

if (incoming == 'P') //If user has selected Play
Mode

Play();

}
```

Working of Record and Play Robotic ARM

Make the association as appeared in the circuit chart and transfer the code that is given underneath. Power your Arduino Nano however the USB port of your PC and open the sequential screen you will be invited with this introduction message.

Presently enter R in the sequential screen and press enter. Note that at the base of the sequential screen Newline ought to be chosen. Once entered the bot will get into Recording mode and you will the accompanying screen.

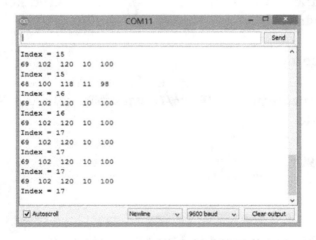

The data appeared here can be utilized for troubleshooting. The numbers beginning structure 69 are the present position of servo engine 0 to engine 5. The record esteems are for the cluster size. Note that the exhibit that we are utilizing has a cutoff of 700 so we have total account the developments before we surpass that limit. After the account is finished we can enter P in the sequential screen and press enter and we will be taken to the Play mode and the sequential screen will show the accompanying.

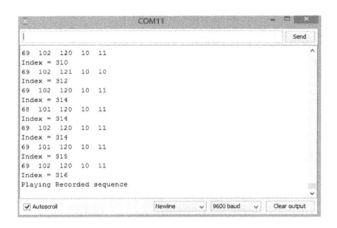

Inside the Play mode the robot will rehash similar developments that were done in the account mode. These developments will be executed over and over until you intrude on it through the Serial screen.

Expectation you comprehended the task and appreciated structure it. You can utilize this bot and fabricate more things over it. I am wanting to give it some vision utilizing Raspberry Pi and Open CV and check what it can do. What are your thoughts? Leave them in the remark segment and I will be glad to get notification from you.

Code

```
/*
  Robotic ARM with Record and Play option using Arduino
*/
#include <Servo.h> //Servo header file
//Declare object for 5 Servo Motors
Servo Servo_0;
Servo Servo_1;
Servo Servo_2;
Servo Servo_3;
Servo Gripper;
//Global Variable Declaration
int S0_pos, S1_pos, S2_pos, S3_pos, G_pos;
int P_S0_pos, P_S1_pos, P_S2_pos, P_S3_pos, P_G_pos;
int C_S0_pos, C_S1_pos, C_S2_pos, C_S3_pos, C_G_pos;
int POT_0,POT_1,POT_2,POT_3,POT_4;
int saved_data[700]; //Array for saving recorded data
int array_index=0;
char incoming = 0;
int action_pos;
int action_servo;
void setup() {
Serial.begin(9600); //Serial Monitor for Debugging
//Declare the pins to which the Servo Motors are connected to
```

```
Servo_0.attach(3);
Servo_1.attach(5);
Servo_2.attach(6);
Servo_3.attach(9);
Gripper.attach(10);
//Write the servo motors to initial position
Servo_0.write(70);
Servo_1.write(100);
Servo_2.write(110);
Servo_3.write(10);
Gripper.write(10);
Serial.println("Press 'R' to Record and 'P' to play"); //
Instruct the user
}
void Read_POT() //Function to read the Analog value
form POT and map it to Servo value
{
  POT_0 = analogRead(A0); POT_1 = analogRead(A1);
POT_2 = analogRead(A2); POT_3 = analogRead(A3);
POT_4 = analogRead(A4); //Read the Analog values
form all five POT
  S0_pos = map(POT_0,0,1024,10,170); //Map it for
1st Servo (Base motor)
  S1_pos = map(POT_1,0,1024,10,170); //Map it for
2nd Servo (Hip motor)
  S2_pos = map(POT_2,0,1024,10,170); //Map it for
3rd Servo (Shoulder motor)
  S3_pos = map(POT_3,0,1024,10,170); //Map it for
4th Servo (Neck motor)
  G_pos = map(POT_4,0,1024,10,170); //Map it for
```

5th Servo (Gripper motor)
}
void Record() //Function to Record the movements of the Robotic Arm
{
Read_POT(); //Read the POT values for 1st time
//Save it in a variable to compare it later
  P_S0_pos = S0_pos;
  P_S1_pos = S1_pos;
  P_S2_pos = S2_pos;
  P_S3_pos = S3_pos;
  P_G_pos = G_pos;

Read_POT(); //Read the POT value for 2nd time

  if (P_S0_pos == S0_pos) //If 1st and 2nd value are same
  {
  Servo_0.write(S0_pos); //Control the servo

   if (C_S0_pos != S0_pos) //If the POT has been turned
   {
     saved_data[array_index] = S0_pos + 0; //Save the new position to the array. Zero is added for zeroth motor (for understading purpose)
     array_index++; //Increase the array index
   }

```
    C_S0_pos = S0_pos; //Saved the previous value to
check if the POT has been turned
    }
//Similarly repeat for all 5 servo Motors
    if(P_S1_pos == S1_pos)
    {
    Servo_1.write(S1_pos);

    if(C_S1_pos != S1_pos)
    {
    saved_data[array_index] = S1_pos + 1000; //1000 is
added for 1st servo motor as differentiator
    array_index++;
    }

    C_S1_pos = S1_pos;
    }
    if(P_S2_pos == S2_pos)
    {
    Servo_2.write(S2_pos);

    if(C_S2_pos != S2_pos)
    {
    saved_data[array_index] = S2_pos + 2000; //2000 is
added for 2nd servo motor as differentiator
    array_index++;
```

```
        }


    C_S2_pos = S2_pos;
        }
    if (P_S3_pos == S3_pos)
    {
    Servo_3.write(S3_pos);


        if (C_S3_pos != S3_pos)
    {
        saved_data[array_index] = S3_pos + 3000; //3000 is
added for 3rd servo motor as differentiater
        array_index++;
    }


    C_S3_pos = S3_pos;
        }
    if (P_G_pos == G_pos)
    {
    Gripper.write(G_pos);


        if (C_G_pos != G_pos)
    {
        saved_data[array_index] = G_pos + 4000; //4000 is
added for 4th servo motor as differentiator
        array_index++;
    }
```

```
        C_G_pos = G_pos;
    }


    //Print the value for debugging
        Serial.print(S0_pos);        Serial.print("        ");
Serial.print(S1_pos);        Serial.print("        ");    Ser-
ial.print(S2_pos);        Serial.print("        ");        Ser-
ial.print(S3_pos);    Serial.print("    ");    Serial.printl-
n(G_pos);
        Serial.print ("Index = "); Serial.println (array_index);
        delay(100);
    }
void Play() //Functon to play the recorded move-
ments on the Robotic ARM
    {
        for  (int  Play_action=0;  Play_action<array_in-
dex; Play_action++) //Navigate through every saved
element in the array
        {
        action_servo = saved_data[Play_action] / 1000; //
The fist character of the array element is split for
knowing the servo number
        action_pos = saved_data[Play_action] % 1000; //
The last three characters of the array element is split
to know the servo postion
        switch(action_servo){ //Check which servo motor
should be controlled
        case 0: //If zeroth motor
```

```
      Servo_0.write(action_pos);
    break;
      case 1://If 1st motor
    Servo_1.write(action_pos);
    break;
      case 2://If 2nd motor
    Servo_2.write(action_pos);
    break;
      case 3://If 3rd motor
    Servo_3.write(action_pos);
    break;
      case 4://If 4th motor
    Gripper.write(action_pos);
    break;
    }
    delay(50);


  }
}
void loop() {
if (Serial.available() > 1) //If something is received
from serial monitor
{
incoming = Serial.read();
if(incoming == 'R')
Serial.println("Robotic Arm Recording Started......");
if(incoming == 'P')
Serial.println("Playing Recorded sequence");
}
```

```
if (incoming == 'R') //If user has selected Record mode
Record();
if (incoming == 'P') //If user has selected Play Mode
Play();
}
```

3.INTERFACING LABVIEW WITH ARDUINO

In past article Getting Started with LabVIEW, we have seen about LabVIEW as well as how it tends to be graphically modified and executed in PC (programming level). Presently in this article we find out about How to Interface LabVIEW with Arduino Board.

Requirements

To interface LabVIEW with Arduino, you require coming up next programming's and hardware's,

- LabVIEW (programming)

- NI VISA (programming)

- VI parcel supervisor (programming)

- Arduino IDE (programming)

- **LINX**, (this will be accessible inside VI bundle director, open VI bundle supervisor and quest for it, double tap on it. You will reach to an establishment window. Snap introduce catch unmistakable to you in that window.)

- **LabVIEW Interface for Arduino**, this will be accessible inside VI bundle administrator, open VI bundle chief and quest for it, double tap on it. You will reach to an establishment window. Snap introduce catch obvious to you in that window, as demonstrated as follows

Why we interface Arduino with LabVIEW?

As of now told in past article, LabVIEW is a graph-ical programming language. Arduino program is com-prised of lines of codes however when we interface LabVIEW with Arduino, lines of codes are decreased

Arduino Interesting projects like 3D Printing and piano tones

into a pictorial program, which is straightforward and execution time is diminished into half.

LED Blink with Arduino & LabVIEW

- Dispatch the LabVIEW.

- To dispatch LabVIEW allude past article.

- Presently start graphical coding.

- In Block graph window, right snap select **Makerhub >> LINX >> Open**, drag and drop the Open box. At that point make a control by right tapping the primary wire tip and choosing Create >> Control. In this way made a Serial port.

Anbazhagan k

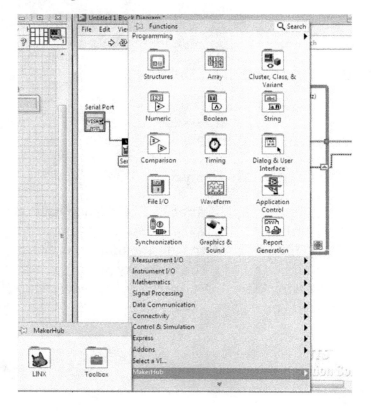

- In Block chart window, right click and select **Makerhub >> LINX >> Close**. Drag and drop Close.

- In Block graph window, right click as well as select **Makerhub >> LINX >> Digital >>Write**. Drag as well as drop Write. At that point make a controls on second and third tip of wires by right clicking each independently and choosing Create >> Control. Therefore made a DO channel and Output Value.

- In Block graph window, right snap and select **Structures >> While circle.** Drag the While circle over the Digital compose. At that point make a Shift register by right tapping on the While circle.

- In Block outline window, right click and select **Makerhub >> LINX >> Utilities >> Loop rate.** Drag and drop it inside the While circle.

- In Block graph window, right snap select **Boolean >> or.** Drag and drop or inside the While circle.

- In Block chart window, right snap and select **Timing >> Wait(ms).** Drag and drop Wait(ms) into the While circle and make a consistent for it by right tapping on the wire tip which is left most to the Wait(ms) and select **Create >> Constant.**

- In Front board window, right click and select **Boolean >> Stop catch.** Presently stop catch shows up in the Block outline window. Drag and drop it inside the While circle.

- Presently by associating all these made squares utilizing wiring associations, you can fabricate the Graphical LED squint program to interface with your Arduino equipment.

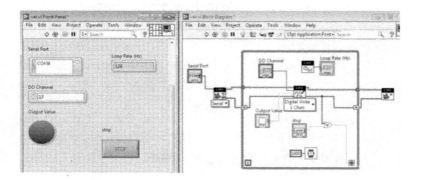

Connect the LabVIEW code with Arduino

- Subsequent to building the graphical code, select **Tools >> Makerhub >> LINX >> LINX Firmware wizard**.

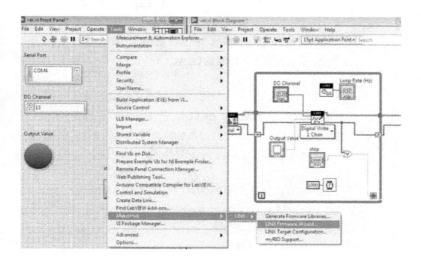

- Presently LINX Firmware wizard window open's, in that select Arduino as Device Family; Arduino Uno as Device type ; Serial/USB as Firmware Upload Method. At that point click Next.

- At that point interface the Arduino board to your PC utilizing Arduino USB link.

- Presently in Next window select the Arduino port by clicking to the drop down rundown. Select COM4. At that point click Next twice.

- At that point snap Finish catch.

- Presently you have arrangement the sequential port and interfaced Arduino board with LabVIEW.

Run the Program

- Presently select the Continuously Run Icon, at that point in the front board window select the port and enter the computerized stick.

- At that point by exchanging the Output Value (which goes about as an On and Off switch), you can see the in-fabricated LED of the Arduino board squinting till the Output

Value is killed.

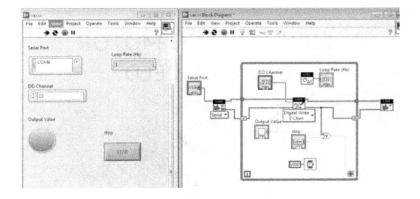

4.DIY ARDUINO MOTOR DRIVER SHIELD

DIY
Arduino
Motor Driver
Shield

In this DIY session, we make an Arduino Motor Driver Shield to drive DC engines, stepper engine and Servo Motor. Perfect with Arduino UNO and Arduino Mega, this engine driver shield can work 4 DC engines or 1 stepper engine and 2 servo engines one after another. Here two L293D Motor Driver ICs are utilized for driving engines and a 8-piece move register for controlling them.

Components Required

- Motor Driver IC L293D -2

- 74HC595 Shift Resistor -1
- 104 capacitors -5
- 3 Pin Terminal Block -5
- Push button -1
- SMD LED -1
- 1k – resistor -1
- PCB (ordered from JLCPCB) -1
- Resistor network 10k -1
- Burg sticks male
- Arduino Uno
- Power supply

Arduino Motor Driver Shield Circuit

This Arduino engine driver shield can be utilized to construct DC or stepper engine based tasks like a Robotic Arm, Line Follower, land burglars, labyrinth devotees and a lot more ventures. This board can be constrained by utilizing Arduino like Arduino UNO, Arduino Mega and comparable sheets. It has screw terminal for conncecting engines wires. L293D engine driver is motioned by utilizing a move register 74HC595 and the move register is motioned by utilizing the Arduino. It has jumper pins to choose either 12v Power to Motors or 5v capacity to engines.

Anbazhagan k

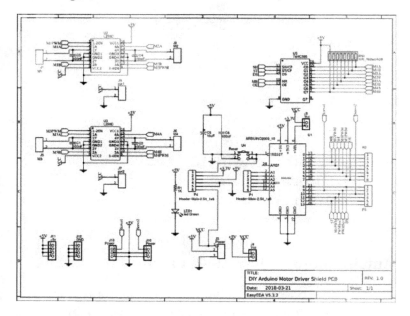

Pin Mapping:

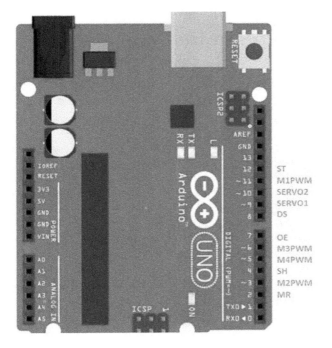

Here

- ST, DS, OE, SH, and MR is utilized for driving Shift Register

- M1PWM, M2PWM, M3PWM, and M4PWM are utilized for controlling DC engine speed. On the off chance that DC engine speed controlling isn't essential make these pins HIGH.

- SERVO 1 and SERVO 2 for Servo Motors.

With this shield, making engine based tasks are too

simple with Arduino. You simply need to fix the shield over Arduino and control engines utilizing this shield. You can utilize the given code (at last) or utilize your very own code for controlling the engines as indicated by your application.

You can likewise get the hang of interfacing of every one of these engines and move register with Arduino in our past articles without utilizing the Motor Driver shield:

- Interfacing Stepper Motor with Arduino UNO

- Controlling Multiple Servo Motor with Arduino

- ?DC Motor Control utilizing Arduino

- ?How to Use Shift Register 74HC595 with Arduino Uno

Circuit and PCB Design using EasyEDA

To plan this Arduino Motor Driver Shield, we have picked the online EDA apparatus called EasyEDA. I have recently utilized EasyEDA commonly and thought that it was an incredible online apparatus to use since it has an enormous gathering of impressions and it is open-source. In the wake of planning the PCB we can arrange the PCB tests by their minimal effort . Besides, they likewise offer segment sourcing administration where they have an enormous supply of electronic segments and clients can arrange the required segments alongside the PCB sheets.

While structuring your circuits and PCBs with EasyEDA, you can make your circuit and PCB plans open so different clients can duplicate or alter them and can take profit by your work, we have made the Circuit and PCB design open for this task, accessible at the underneath connection:

You can see any Layer (Top, Bottom, Topsilk, bottomsilk and so forth) of the PCB by choosing the layer structure the 'Layers' Window. You can likewise see the PCB, how it will take care of manufacture utilizing the Photo View catch in EasyEDA:

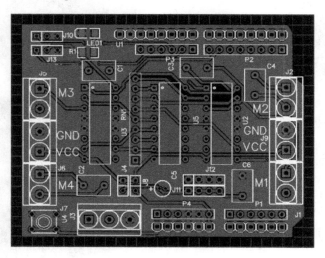

Calculating and Ordering Samples online

In the wake of finishing the structure of this Arduino Motor Shield, you can arrange the PCB through . To arrange the PCB from JLCPCB, you need Gerber File. To download Gerber records of your PCB simply click the Fabrication Output catch in EasyEDA supervisor page, at that point download from the EasyEDA PCB request page.

Presently go to and click on Quote Now or Buy Now catch, at that point you can choose the quantity of PCBs you need to arrange, what number of copper layers you need, the PCB thickness, copper weight, and even the PCB shading, similar to the preview demonstrated as follows:

After you have chosen the majority of the alternatives, click "Spare to Cart" and afterward you will be taken to the page where you can transfer your Gerber File which we have downloaded from EasyEDA. Transfer your Gerber record and snap "Spare to Cart". Lastly click on Checkout Securely to finish your request, at that point you will get your PCBs a couple of days after the fact. They are manufacturing the PCB at low rate which is $2. Their manufacture time is likewise less which is 48 hours with DHL conveyance of 3-5 days, fundamentally you will get your PCBs inside seven days of requesting.

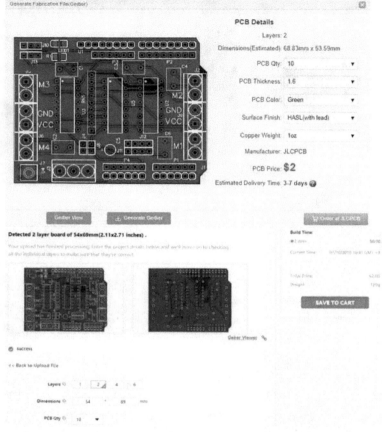

In the wake of requesting the PCB, you can check the Production Progress of your PCB with date and time. You check it by going on Account page and snap on "Generation Progress" interface under the PCB like, appeared in underneath picture.

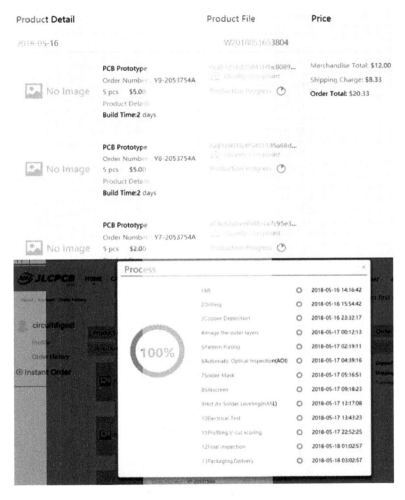

Following couple of long periods of requesting PCB's I got the PCB tests in pleasant bundling as appeared in underneath pictures.

Subsequent to getting these pieces I have mounted all the required segments over the PCB associated it with Arduino for exhibit.

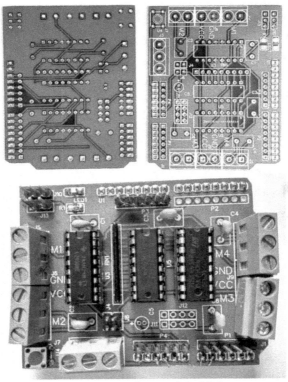

So our Arduino Motor Driver Shield is prepared, and you can straightforwardly utilize it with Arduino to control numerous engines one after another.

Code

```
#include <Servo.h>
Servo myservo;
#define MR 2
#define M2PWM 3
#define SH 4
#define M4PWM 5
#define M3PWM 6
#define OE 7
#define DS 8
#define SERVO1 9
#define SERVO2 10
#define M1PWM 11
#define ST 12

#define M1 0
#define M2 2
#define M3 4
#define M4 6

#define STOP 0
#define CW 1
#define CCW 2

char pAction=0x00;

void setup()
{
 Serial.begin(9600);
 pinMode(MR, OUTPUT);
 pinMode(M2PWM, OUTPUT);
 pinMode(SH, OUTPUT);
 pinMode(M4PWM, OUTPUT);
 pinMode(M3PWM, OUTPUT);
 pinMode(OE, OUTPUT);
```

```
pinMode(DS, OUTPUT);
pinMode(M1PWM, OUTPUT);
pinMode(ST, OUTPUT);
 digitalWrite(M1PWM, HIGH);
 digitalWrite(M2PWM, HIGH);
 digitalWrite(M3PWM, HIGH);
 digitalWrite(M4PWM, HIGH);
 digitalWrite(MR, HIGH);
 digitalWrite(OE, LOW);
 myservo.attach(SERVO1);
 myservo.write(0);
}
void loop()
{
 DriveMotor(M1,CW);
 DriveMotor(M2,CCW);
 DriveMotor(M2,CW);
 DriveMotor(M3,CW);
 DriveMotor(M4,CW);
 myservo.write(0);
 delay(5000);
 DriveMotor(M1,STOP);
 DriveMotor(M2,STOP);
 DriveMotor(M3,STOP);
 DriveMotor(M4,STOP);
 delay(1000);
 DriveMotor(M1,CCW);
 DriveMotor(M2,CCW);
 DriveMotor(M3,CCW);
 DriveMotor(M4,CCW);
```

```
myservo.write(90);
delay(5000);
  DriveMotor(M1,STOP);
DriveMotor(M2,STOP);
DriveMotor(M3,STOP);
DriveMotor(M4,STOP);
delay(1000);
DriveMotor(M1,CW);
DriveMotor(M2,CCW);
DriveMotor(M3,CW);
DriveMotor(M4,CCW);
myservo.write(180);
delay(5000);
  DriveMotor(M1,STOP);
DriveMotor(M2,STOP);
DriveMotor(M3,STOP);
DriveMotor(M4,STOP);
delay(1000);
DriveMotor(M1,CCW);
DriveMotor(M2,CW);
DriveMotor(M3,CCW);
DriveMotor(M4,CW);
myservo.write(90);
delay(5000);
  DriveMotor(M1,STOP);
DriveMotor(M2,STOP);
DriveMotor(M3,STOP);
DriveMotor(M4,STOP);
delay(1000);
DriveMotor(M1,STOP);
DriveMotor(M2,CW);
```

```
DriveMotor(M3,CCW);
DriveMotor(M4,CW);
myservo.write(0);
delay(5000);
  DriveMotor(M1,STOP);
DriveMotor(M2,STOP);
DriveMotor(M3,STOP);
DriveMotor(M4,STOP);
delay(1000);
DriveMotor(M1,STOP);
DriveMotor(M2,STOP);
DriveMotor(M3,CW);
DriveMotor(M4,CCW);
myservo.write(90);
delay(5000);
  DriveMotor(M1,STOP);
DriveMotor(M2,STOP);
DriveMotor(M3,STOP);
DriveMotor(M4,STOP);
delay(1000);
DriveMotor(M1,STOP);
DriveMotor(M2,STOP);
DriveMotor(M3,STOP);
DriveMotor(M4,CCW);
myservo.write(180);
delay(5000);
DriveMotor(M1,STOP);
DriveMotor(M2,STOP);
DriveMotor(M3,STOP);
DriveMotor(M4,STOP);
myservo.write(90);
```

```
 delay(5000);
}
int Action=0;
void DriveMotor(int Motor, int Dir)
{
// Serial.print("Motor :");
// Serial.println(Motor, HEX);
// Serial.print("Action:");
// Serial.println(Action,HEX);
 if(Dir == CW)
 {
  Action|=(1<<Motor);
  Action&=~(1<<Motor+1);
 }
 else if(Dir == CCW)
 {
  Action&=~(1<<Motor);
  Action|=(1<<Motor+1);
 }
  else
 {
    Action&=~(1<<Motor);
    Action&=~(1<<Motor+1);
 }
Serial.print("Action:");
Serial.println(Action, HEX);
 // delay(2000);


 for (int i = 0; i < 8; i++)
```

```
{
 if ((Action << i) & 0x80)
  digitalWrite(DS, HIGH);
 else
  digitalWrite(DS, LOW);
  digitalWrite(SH, HIGH);
  delay(1);
  digitalWrite(SH, LOW);
 }
 digitalWrite(ST, HIGH);
 delay(1);
 digitalWrite(ST, LOW);
 pAction=Action;
}
```

5.INTERFACING FLAME SENSOR WITH ARDUINO TO BUILD A FIRE ALARM SYSTEM

Here we interface Flame Sensor with Arduino and get familiar with every one of the means to construct Fire Alarm System by utilizing Arduino and fire sensor. Fire sensor module has photodiode to distinguish the light and operation amp to control the affectability. It is utilized to distinguish fire and give HIGH signal upon the location. Arduino peruses the sign and gives alert by turning on ringer and LED. Fire sensor utilized here is an IR based fire sensor.

Flame Sensor

A fire locator is a sensor intended to recognize as well as react to the nearness of a fire or fire. Reactions to an identified fire rely upon the establishment, however can incorporate sounding a caution, inactive a fuel line, (for example, a propane or a combustible gas line), and actuating a flame concealment framework.

There are various sorts of fire identification strategies. Some of them are: Ultraviolet indicator, close to IR exhibit identifier, infrared (IR) finder, Infrared warm cameras, UV/IR locator and so on.

At the point when fire consumes it transmits a modest quantity of Infra-red light, this light will be gotten by the Photodiode (IR collector) on the sensor module. At that point we utilize an Op-Amp to check for change in voltage over the IR Receiver, so that if a flame is distinguished the yield stick (DO) will give 0V(LOW) and if the is no flame the yield stick will be 5V(HIGH).

In this undertaking we are utilizing an IR based fire sensor. It depends on the YG1006 sensor which is a fast and high touchy NPN silicon phototransistor. It can distinguish infrared light with a wavelength going from 700nm to 1000nm as well as its recognition edge is about 60°. Fire sensor module comprises of a photodiode (IR collector), resistor, capacitor, potentiometer, and LM393 comparator in a coordinated circuit. The affectability can be balanced by changing the on board potentiometer. Working voltage is somewhere in the range of 3.3v and 5v DC, with a computerized yield. Rationale high on the yield demonstrates nearness of fire or fire. Rationale low on yield demonstrates nonattendance of fire or fire.

The following is the Pin Description of Flame sensor Module:

Pin	Description
Vcc	3.3 – 5V power supply
GND	Ground
Dout	Digital output

Applications of flame sensors

- Hydrogen stations

- Ignition screens for burners

- Oil and gas pipelines
- Car fabricating offices
- Atomic offices
- Flying machine shelters
- Turbine fenced in areas

Components Required

- Arduino Uno (any Arduino board can be used)
- Flame sensor
- LED
- Buzzer
- Resistor
- Jumper wires

Circuit Diagram

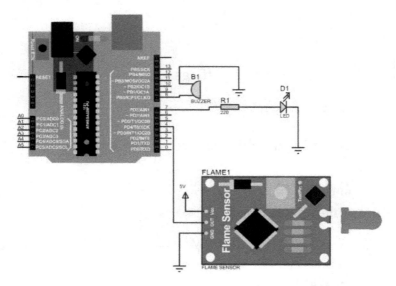

Working of Flame Sensor with Arduino

Arduino Uno is an public source microcontroller board dependent on ATmega328p microcontroller. It has 14 advanced pins (out of which 6 pins can be utilized as PWM yields), 6 simple contributions, on board voltage controllers and so on. Arduino Uno has 32KB of glimmer memory, 2KB of SRAM and 1KB of EEPROM. It works at the clock recurrence of 16MHz. Arduino Uno bolsters Serial, I2C, SPI correspondence for speaking with different gadgets. The table beneath demonstrates the specialized determination of Arduino Uno.

Microcontroller	ATmega328p
Operating voltage	5V
Input Voltage	7-12V (recommended)
Digital I/O pins	14
Analog pins	6
Flash memory	32KB
SRAM	2KB
EEPROM	1KB
Clock speed	16MHz

The fire sensor identifies the nearness of flame or fire dependent on the Infrared (IR) wavelength radiated by the fire. It gives rationale 1 as yield if fire is recognized, else it gives rationale 0 as yield. Arduino Uno checks the rationale level on the yield stick of the sensor and performs further undertakings, for example, actuating the signal and LED, sending an alarm message.

Additionally, check our other alarm ventures:

- Alarm utilizing Thermistor

- Alarm System utilizing AVR Microcontroller

- Arduino Based Fire Fighting Robot

Code explanation

The total Arduino code for this venture is given in the part of the arrangement. The code is part into little significant lumps and clarified underneath.

In this piece of the code we will characterize pins for Flame sensor, LED and bell which are associated with

Arduino. Fire sensor is associated with advanced stick 4 of Arduino. Bell is associated with advanced stick 8 of Arduino. Driven is associated with computerized stick 7 of Arduino.

Variable "flame_detected" is utilized for putting away the advanced worth read out from fire sensor. In light of this worth we will identify the nearness of fire.

```
int buzzer = 8 ;

int LED = 7 ;

int flame_sensor = 4 ;

int flame_detected ;
```

In this piece of the code, we are going to set the status of computerized pins of Arduino and design

Baud rate for Serial correspondence with PC for showing status of fire recognition circuit.

```
void setup()

{

  Serial.begin(9600);
```

```
pinMode(buzzer, OUTPUT);

pinMode(LED, OUTPUT);

pinMode(flame_sensor, INPUT);

}
```

This line of code peruses the advanced yield from fire sensor and stores it in the variable "flame_detected".

```
flame_detected = digitalRead(flame_sensor);
```

In light of the worth put away in "flame_detected", we need to turn on the ringer and LED. In this piece of the code, we analyze the worth put away in "flame_detected" with 0 or 1.

On the off chance that its equivalent to 1, it demonstrates that fire has been distinguished. We need to turn on ringer and LED and afterward show an alarm message in Serial screen of Arduino IDE.

In the event that its equivalent to 0, at that point it demonstrates that no fire has been recognized so we need to mood killer LED and signal. This procedure is rehashed each second to differentiate the nearness of flame or fire.

```
if (flame_detected == 1)

{

    Serial.println("Flame detected...! take action immediately.");

    digitalWrite(buzzer, HIGH);

    digitalWrite(LED, HIGH);

    delay(200);

    digitalWrite(LED, LOW);

    delay(200);

}

else

{

    Serial.println("No flame detected. stay cool");

    digitalWrite(buzzer, LOW);

    digitalWrite(LED, LOW);
```

```
}

delay(1000);
```

We have manufactured a putting out fires robot dependent on this idea, which consequently identify the flame and siphon out the water to put down the flame.

Check the total code is given underneath.

Code

```
int buzzer = 8;
int LED = 7;
int flame_sensor = 4;
int flame_detected;
void setup()
{
 Serial.begin(9600);
 pinMode(buzzer, OUTPUT);
 pinMode(LED, OUTPUT);
 pinMode(flame_sensor, INPUT);
}
void loop()
{
 flame_detected = digitalRead(flame_sensor);
 if(flame_detected == 1)
 {
   Serial.println("Flame detected...! take action immediately.");
```

```
digitalWrite(buzzer, HIGH);
digitalWrite(LED, HIGH);
delay(200);
digitalWrite(LED, LOW);
delay(200);
}
else
{
Serial.println("No flame detected. stay cool");
digitalWrite(buzzer, LOW);
digitalWrite(LED, LOW);
}
delay(1000);
}
```

6.REED SWITCH INTERFACING WITH ARDUINO

Reed switch is utilized in huge numbers of the genuine applications, for example, attractive entryway switch, PCs, cell phones and so forth. Here, we find out about Reed Switch as well as direct you to interface a reed switch with arduino.

Reed Switch

Reed switch is essentially an electrical switch which

is worked when an attractive field is brought close to it. It was imagined by W. B. Ellwood in 1936 at chime research centers. It is comprised of two little metal pieces kept inside a glass tube under vacuum. In an average reed switch two metal pieces will be made of a ferromagnetic material as well as secured with rhodium or ruthenium to give them long life. The switch will be enacted when there is a nearness of attractive field around the switch.

The glass nook of the two metal pieces shield them from earth, dust and different particles. Reed switch can be worked in any condition, for example, condition where combustible gas is available or condition where erosion would influence open switch contacts.

There are two sorts of reed switch.

· Typically open reed switch

· Typically shut reed switch

In typically open reed switch, switch is open without attractive field and it is shut within the sight of attractive field. Under the nearness of attractive field, two metal contacts inside the glass cylinder pull in one another to reach.

In regularly shut reed switch, switch is shut without attractive field and it is open within the sight of attractive field.

Applications of Reed switch

- Utilized in phone trade

- In PCs to put the screen on rest if the top is shut

- Utilized in window and entryway sensors in criminal caution framework

Components Required

- Reed switch
- Arduino Uno
- LED
- Resistors
- Connecting wires
- Magnet

Arduino Reed Switch Circuit Diagram

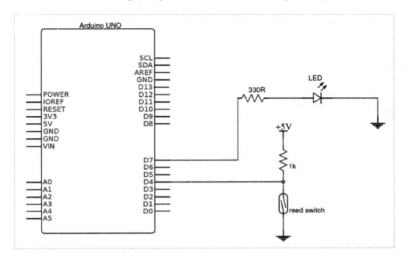

Working of Reed Switch with Arduino

Arduino Uno is an public source microcontroller board dependent on ATmega328p microcontroller. It has 14 advanced pins (out of which 6 pins can be utilized as PWM yields), 6 simple contributions, on board voltage controllers and so forth. Arduino Uno has 32KB of blaze memory, 2KB of SRAM and 1KB of EEPROM. It works at the clock recurrence of 16MHz. Arduino Uno bolsters Serial, I2C, SPI correspondence for speaking with different gadgets. The table beneath demonstrates the specialized particular of Arduino Uno.

Microcontroller	ATmega328p
Operating voltage	5V

Input Voltage	7-12V (recommended)
Digital I/O pins	14
Analog pins	6
Flash memory	32KB
SRAM	2KB
EEPROM	1KB
Clock speed	16MHz

To interface reed switch with Arduino we have to manufacture a voltage divider circuit as appeared in the figure underneath. Vo is +5V when the switch is open and 0V when the switch is shut. We are utilizing a regularly open reed switch in this venture. Switch is shut within the sight of attractive field and it is open without attractive field.

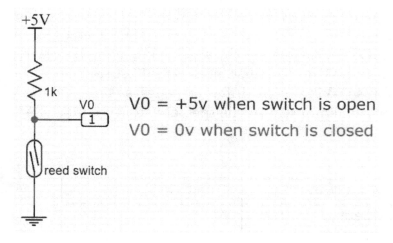

VO = +5v when switch is open

VO = 0v when switch is closed

Code explanation

The total code for this Arduino reed switch venture is given toward the part of the arrangement. The code is part into little important pieces and clarified underneath.

In this piece of the code we need to characterize sticks on which Reed switch and LED which is associated with Arduino. Reed switch is associated with computerized stick 4 of Arduino and LED is associated with advanced stick 7 of Arduino through a present constraining resistor. The variable "reed_status" is utilized to hold the status of reed switch.

```
int LED = 7;
```

```
int reed_switch = 4;

int reed_status;
```

In this piece of the code, we need to set status of pins on which drove as well as reed switch is associated. Stick number 4 is set as information and stick number 7 is set as yield.

```
void setup()

{

  pinMode(LED, OUTPUT);

  pinMode(reed_switch, INPUT);

}
```

Next, we need to peruse the status of reed switch. On the off chance that it is equivalent to 1, switch is open and LED is killed. On the off chance that it is equivalent to 0, switch is shut and we need to turn on LED. This procedure is rehashed each second. This assignment is cultivated with this piece of the code beneath.

```
void loop()
```

```
{

    reed_status = digitalRead(reed_switch);

    if (reed_status == 1)

      digitalWrite(LED, LOW);

    else

      digitalWrite(LED, HIGH);

    delay(1000);

}
```

So as you have seen its extremely simple to utilize Reed Switch with Arduino.

Code

```
int LED = 7;
int reed_switch = 4;
int reed_status;
void setup()
{
 pinMode(LED, OUTPUT);
 pinMode(reed_switch, INPUT);
}
void loop()
```

```
{
reed_status = digitalRead(reed_switch);
if(reed_status == 1)
 digitalWrite(LED, LOW);
else
 digitalWrite(LED, HIGH);
delay(1000);
}
```

7.WHAT IS ROTARY ENCODER AND HOW TO USE IT WITH ARDUINO

A Rotary encoder is an info gadget which encourages the client to connect with a framework. It looks increasingly like a Radio potentiometer however it yields a train of heartbeats which makes its application novel. At the point when the handle of the Encoder is pivoted it turns in type of little advances which causes it to be utilized for stepper/Servo engine controlling, exploring through a succession of menu and Increasing/diminishing the estimation of a number and substantially more.

Here we will find out about the various kinds of Rotary Encoders as well as how it work. We will likewise interface it with Arduino and control the estimation of a number by turning the Encoder and show its incentive on a 16*2 LCD screen. Toward the part of the arrangement you will be alright with utilizing a Rotary Encoder for your tasks. So we should begin...

Materials Required

> ➤ Arduino UNO
> ➤ Rotary Encoder (KY-040)
> ➤ Potentiometer 10k
> ➤ 16*2 Alphanumeric LCD
> ➤ Connecting wires
> ➤ Breadboard

How does a Rotary Encoder Work?

A Rotary Encoder is an electromechanical transducer, which means it changes over mechanical developments into electronic heartbeats. It comprises of a handle which when turns will move bit by bit and produce an arrangement of heartbeat trains with pre-characterized width for each progression. There are numerous kinds of Encoders each with its own working system, we will find out about the sorts later yet until further notice let us focus just on the KY040 Incremental Encoder since we are utilizing it for our instructional exercise.

The inside mechanical structure for the Encoder is demonstrated as follows. It fundamentally comprises of a round plate (dark shading) with conductive cushions (copper shading) put over this roundabout circle. These conductive cushions are set at an equivalent separation as demonstrated as follows. The Output pins are fixed over this roundabout circle, so that when the handle is pivots the conductive cushions get in contact with the yield pins. Here there are two yield stick, Output An and Output B as appeared in the figure beneath.

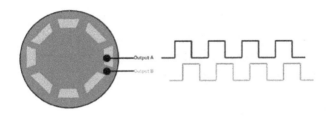

The yield waveform created by the Output stick An and Output B is appear in blue and green shading individually. At the point when the conductive cushion is legitimately under the stick it goes high coming about it on schedule and when the conductive cushion moves away the stick goes low coming about in off time of the waveform appeared previously. Presently, in the event that we tally the quantity of heartbeats we will almost certainly decide what number of steps the Encoder has been moved.

Presently the inquiry may emerge that, for what reason do we need two heartbeat signals when one is sufficient to check the quantity of steps taken while turning the handle. This is on the grounds that we have to distinguish in which bearing the handle has been turned. In the event that you investigate the two heartbeats you can see that the two of them are 90° out of stage. Subsequently when the handle is turned clockwise the yield A will go high first as well as when the handle is pivoted against clockwise the Output B will go high first.

Types of Rotary Encoder

There are numerous kinds of rotating encoder in the market the originator can pick one as per his application. The most widely recognized sorts are recorded underneath

- ❖ Gradual Encoder

- ❖ Supreme Encoder

- ❖ Attractive Encoder

- ❖ Optical Encoder

- ❖ Laser Encoder

These encoders are arranged dependent on the Output sign and detecting innovation, the Incremental

Encoder and Absolute Encoders are grouped dependent on Output signal and the Magnetic, Optical and Laser Encoder are characterized dependent on Sensing Technology. The Encoder utilized here is an Incremental kind Encoder.

KY-040 Rotary Encoder Pinout and description

The pinouts of the KY-040 Incremental sort revolving encoder is demonstrated as follows

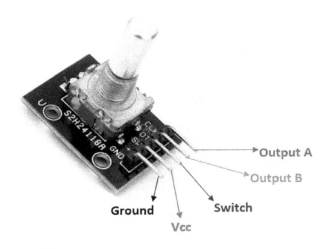

The initial two pins (Ground and Vcc) is utilized to control the Encoder, normally +5V supply is utilized. Aside from turning the handle in clock insightful and hostile to clockwise heading, the encoder likewise has a switch (Active low) which can be squeezed by squeezing the handle inside. The sign from this switch is acquired through the stick 3 (Switch). At long last it has the two yield pins which produce the waveforms as of now examined previously. Presently let us figure out how to interface it with Arduino.

Arduino Rotary Encoder Circuit Diagram

The total circuit graph for Interfacing Revolving Encoder with Arduino is appeared in the image underneath

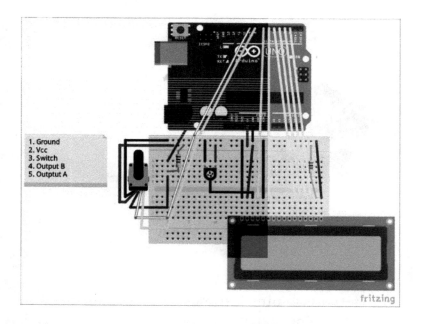

1. Ground
2. Vcc
3. Switch
4. Output B
5. Outptut A

The Rotary Encoder has 5 sticks in the request appeared in the mark above. The initial two pins are Ground and Vcc which is associated with the Ground and +5V stick of the Arduino. The switch of the encoder is associated with advanced stick D10 and is likewise pulled high however a 1k resistor. The two yield pins are associated with D9 and D8 individually.

To show the estimation of the variable which will be expanded or diminished by pivoting the Rotary encoder we need a presentation module. The one utilized here is regularly accessible 16*2 Alpha numeric LCD show. We have associated the presentation to be worked in 4-piece mode and have fueled it utilizing the +5V stick of Arduino. The Potentiometer is utilized to modify the differentiation of the LCD show. In the event that you need to find out about Interfacing LCD show with Arduino pursue the connection. The total circuit can be based over a breadboard, my looked something like this beneath once every one of the associations were finished.

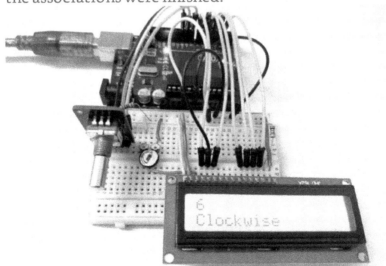

Programming your Arduino for Rotary Encoder

It is genuinely simple as well as straight forward to program the Arduino board for interfacing a Turning Encoder with it on the off chance that you had comprehended the working standard of a Rotary Encoder. We essentially need to peruse the quantity of heartbeat to decide what number of turns the encoder has made and check which heartbeat went high first to discover in which heading the encoder was pivoted. In this instructional exercise we will show the number that is being addition or decrement on the principal column of the LCD and the course of the Encoder in the subsequent line. The total program for doing likewise can be found at the base of this page, it doesn't require any library. Presently, how about we split the program into little pieces to comprehend the working.

Since we have utilized a LCD show, we incorporate the Liquid precious stone library which is as a matter of course present in the Arduino IDE. At that point we characterize pins for interfacing LCD with Arduino. At long last we initialise the LCD show on those pins.

```
#include <LiquidCrystal.h> //Default Arduino
LCD Library is included

const int rs = 7, en = 6, d4 = 5, d5 = 4, d6 = 3, d7 =
```

```
2; //Mention the pin number for LCD connection

LiquidCrystal lcd(rs, en, d4, d5, d6, d7);

lcd.begin(16, 2); //Initialise 16*2 LCD
```

Next inside the arrangement work, we show an initial message on the LCD screen, and after that hang tight for 2 seconds with the goal that that message is client comprehensible. This is to guarantee that the LCD is working appropriately.

```
lcd.print(" Rotary Encoder "); //Intro Message line 1

lcd.setCursor(0, 1);

lcd.print(" With Arduino "); //Intro Message line 2

delay(2000);

lcd.clear();
```

The Rotary encoder has three yield pins which will be an INPUT pins for the Arduino. These three pins are the Switch, Output An and Output B separately. These are pronounced as Input utilizing the pinMode work as demonstrated as follows.

```
//pin Mode declaration

 pinMode (Encoder_OuputA, INPUT);

 pinMode (Encoder_OuputB, INPUT);

 pinMode (Encoder_Switch, INPUT);
```

Inside the void arrangement work, we read the status of the yield A stick to check the last status of the stick. We will at that point utilize this data to contrast with the new esteem with check which stick (Output An or Output B) has gone high.

```
Previous_Output      =      digitalRead(Encoder_OuputA); //Read the inital value of Output A
```

At last inside the primary circle work, we need to look at the estimation of Output An and Output B with the Previous Output to check which one goes high first. This should be possible by just contrasting the estimation of current yield of An and B with the past yield as demonstrated as follows.

```
if  (digitalRead(Encoder_OuputA)  !=  Previ-
```

```
ous_Output)

{

    if  (digitalRead(Encoder_OuputB)  !=  Previ-
ous_Output)

    {

        Encoder_Count ++;

        lcd.clear();

        lcd.print(Encoder_Count);

        lcd.setCursor(0, 1);

        lcd.print("Clockwise");

    }
```

In the above code the second if condition gets executed whenever Output B has transformed from the past yield. All things considered the estimation of the encoder variable is increased and the LCD shows that the encoder is pivoted clockwise way. Additionally if that if condition falls flat, in the consequent else condition we decrement the variable and show that the encoder is pivoted the anticlockwise way. The code for the equivalent is demonstrated as follows.

```
else

{

    Encoder_Count--;

    lcd.clear();

    lcd.print(Encoder_Count);

    lcd.setCursor(0, 1);

    lcd.print("Anti - Clockwise");

}

}
```

At long last, toward the part of the bargain circle we need to refresh the past yield an incentive with the present yield esteem so the circle can be rehashed with a similar rationale. The accompanying code does likewise

```
Previous_Output        =        digitalRead(Encoder_OuputA);
```

Another discretionary thing is to check if the switch on the Encoder is squeezed. This can be observed by checking the switch stick on the revolving coder. This stick is a functioning low stick, implying that it will go low when the catch is squeezed. If not squeezed the stick remains high, we likewise have utilized a destroy up resistor to ensure the stays high when switch isn't squeezed in this way abstaining from drifting point condition.

```
if (digitalRead(Encoder_Switch) == 0)

{

    lcd.clear();

    lcd.setCursor(0, 1);

    lcd.print("Switch pressed");

}
```

Working of Rotary Encoder with Arduino

When the equipment and code is prepared, simply transfer the code to the Arduino block and power the Arduino Board. You can either control it through the USB link or utilize a 12V connector. At the point when fueled the LCD should show the introduction message and after that get clear. Presently turn the rotational encoder and you should see the worth start augmented or decremented dependent on the course you pivot. The subsequent line will demonstrate to you if the encoder is being pivoted in clockwise or hostile to clockwise bearing. The image beneath demonstrates the equivalent

Likewise when the catch is squeezed, the subsequent line will show that the catch is squeezed. This is only an example program to interface the Encoder with Arduino and check on the off chance that it is filling in true to form. When you arrive you must have the option to use the encoder for any of your undertakings and program as needs be.

Expectation you have comprehended the instructional exercise and things filled in as it should.

Code

```
/*
* Interfacing Rotary Encoder with Arduino
*
* Power LCD and Rotary encoder from the +5V pin of
Arduino
* LCD RS -> pin 7
* LCD EN -> pin 6
* LCD D4 -> pin 5
* LCD D5 -> pin 4
* LCD D6 -> pin 3
* LCD D7 -> pin 2
* Encoder Switch -> pin 10
* Encoder Output A -> pin 9
* Encoder Output B -> pin 8
*/
int Encoder_OuputA = 9;
int Encoder_OuputB = 8;
int Encoder_Switch = 10;

int Previous_Output;
int Encoder_Count;

#include <LiquidCrystal.h>  //Default Arduino LCD
Librarey is included
const int rs = 7, en = 6, d4 = 5, d5 = 4, d6 = 3, d7 = 2; //
Mention the pin number for LCD connection
LiquidCrystal lcd(rs, en, d4, d5, d6, d7);

void setup() {
lcd.begin(16, 2); //Initialise 16*2 LCD
```

```
  lcd.print(" Rotary Encoder "); //Intro Message line 1
lcd.setCursor(0, 1);
lcd.print(" With Arduino "); //Intro Message line 2
 delay(2000);
lcd.clear();
//pin Mode declaration
pinMode (Encoder_OuputA, INPUT);
pinMode (Encoder_OuputB, INPUT);
pinMode (Encoder_Switch, INPUT);
 Previous_Output       =        digitalRead(Encoder_OuputA); //Read the inital value of Output A
}
void loop() {
 //aVal = digitalRead(pinA);


  if (digitalRead(Encoder_OuputA) != Previous_Output)
 {
  if (digitalRead(Encoder_OuputB) != Previous_Output)
  {
  Encoder_Count ++;
  lcd.clear();
  lcd.print(Encoder_Count);
  lcd.setCursor(0, 1);
  lcd.print("Clockwise");
  }
  else
  {
```

```
      Encoder_Count--;
      lcd.clear();
      lcd.print(Encoder_Count);
      lcd.setCursor(0, 1);
      lcd.print("Anti - Clockwise");
    }
  }
      Previous_Output = digitalRead(Encoder_OuputA);
      if(digitalRead(Encoder_Switch) == 0)
    {
      lcd.clear();
      lcd.setCursor(0, 1);
      lcd.print("Switch pressed");
    }
  }
```

8.WHAT IS BRUSHLESS DC MOTOR (BLDC) AND HOW TO CONTROL IT WITH ARDUINO

Building stuff as well as getting them work, the manner in which we need, has consistently been sheer fun. While that being concurred, constructing stuff that could fly would insubordinately siphon more nervousness among the specialists and equipment tinkerers. Indeed! I am discussing Gliders, Helicopters, Planes and mostly multi-copters. Today it has ended up being anything but difficult to manufacture one all alone because of the network bolster accessible on the web. One regular thing with every one of the things that fly is that they utilize a BLDC engine, so what is this BLDC engine? For what reason do we need it to fly things? What is so exceptional about it? How to purchase the correct engine and interface it with your controller? What is an ESC and for what reason do we use it? In the event that you have questions like these, at that point this instructional exercise is your one stop arrangement.

So fundamentally in this instructional exercise we will control the speed of an A2212/13T Sensorless BLDC outrunner engine (the normally used to manufacture rambles) with a 20A ESC utilizing Arduino.

Materials Required

- ➢ Potentiometer
- ➢ ESC (20A)
- ➢ A2212/13T BLDC Motor
- ➢ Arduino
- ➢ Power Source (12V 20A)

Understanding BLDC Motors

BLDC Motor represents Brush Less DC engine, it is ordinarily utilized in roof fans and electric vehicles because of its smooth activity. In contrast to different engines, the BLDC engines have three wires leaving them and each wire frames its own stage along these

Anbazhagan k

lines given us a three stage Motor. Pause... what!!??

Indeed, in spite of the fact that BLDC engines are viewed as DC engines, they work with the assistance of Pulsed waves. The ESC changes over the DC voltage from the battery into beats and gives it to the 3 wires of the Motor. At some random time just two Phase of the engine will be controlled, with the goal that present enters through one stage and leaves through other. During this procedure the curl inside the engine is invigorated and subsequently the magnets on the rotor adjust itself to the stimulated loop. At that point the following two wires are stimulated by the ESC, this procedure is kept on causing the engine to pivot. The speed of the engine relies upon how quick the loop is invigorated and course of engine relies upon in which request the curls are stimulated. We will study ESC later in this article.

There are numerous sorts of BLDC engines accessible, how about we take a gander at the most well-known arrangements.

In-sprinter and Out-Runner BLDC engine: In sprinter BLDC Motors work like some other engine. That is the pole inside the engine turns while packaging stays fixed. While out sprinter BLDC engines are the exact inverse, the Outer packaging of the engine pivots alongside the pole while the loop inside remains fixed. Out sprinter engines are very preferences in Electric bicycles since the external packaging (the one that pivots) itself is made into a Rim for the tires and consequently a coupling component is maintained a vital good ways from . Additionally the out sprinter engines will in general give more torque than in sprinter types, consequently it turns into a perfect decision in EV and Drones. The one that we are utilizing here is additionally an out sprinter type.

Note: There is another kind of engine called the coreless BLDC engines which are additionally utilized for pocket Drones, they have an alternate working guideline yet until further notice we should skip it for this instructional exercise.

Sensor and Sensorless BLDC Motor: For a BLDC engine to turn with no jolt a criticism is required. That is the ESC needs to know the position and shaft of the magnets in the rotor in order to invigorate the stator agreeing. This data can be procured in two different ways; one is by putting lobby sensor inside the engine. The lobby sensor will identify the magnet and send the data to ESC this sort of engine is known as a Sensord BLDC engine and is utilized in Electric vehicles. The subsequent strategy is by utilizing the back EMF produced by the loops when the magnets cross them, this required not extra equipment or wires the stage wire itself is utilized as an input to check for back EMF. This strategy is utilized in our engine and is regular for automatons and other flying tasks.

Why do Drones and other Multi-copters use BLDC Motors?

There are numerous sorts of cool automatons out there from Quad copter to helicopters and light-weight flyers everything shares one equipment for all intents and purpose. That is the BLDC engines, however why? For what reason do they utilize a BLDC engine which is somewhat costly contrasted with DC Motors?

There are many substantial purposes behind this, one fundamental reason is the torque given by these engines are high which is essential to increase/free push quickly to bring off or land down an automaton. Likewise these engines are accessible as out sprinters which again expands the push of the engines. Another explanation behind select BLDC engine is its smooth vibration less activity, this is extremely perfect to our automaton stable in mid-air.

The ability to weight proportion of a BLDC engine is high. This is significant in light of the fact that the engines utilized on automatons ought to be of high control (fast and high torque) yet should likewise be of less weight. A DC engine which could give a similar torque as well as speed of that of a BLDC engine will be twice as overwhelming as the BLDC engine.

Why do we need an ESC and what is its function?

As we probably am aware each BLDC engine requires a type of controller to change over the DC voltage from the battery into heartbeats to control the stage wires of the engine. This controller is called an ESC which represents Electronic Speed Controller. The fundamental duty of the controller is to invigorate the Phase wires of the BLDC engines in a request with the goal that the engine pivots. This is finished by detecting the back EMF from each wire and invigorate the loop precisely when the magnet crosses the curl. So there is a ton of equipment brightness inside the ESC which is out of the extent of this instructional exercise. In any case, to make reference to a couple of it has speed controller and a battery eliminator circuit.

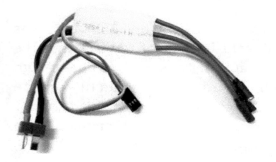

PWM based speed control: The ESC can control the speed of the BLDC engine by perusing the PWM sign gave on the Orange wire. It works particularly like servo engines, the gave PWM sign ought to have a time of 20ms and the obligation cycle can be differed to fluctuate the speed of the BLDC engine. Since a similar rationale additionally applies for the servo engines to control the position we can utilize a similar servo library in our Arduino program. Pick up utilizing Servo with Arduino here.

Battery Eliminator Circuit (BEC): Almost the entirety of ESC's accompanies a Battery eliminator circuit. As the name proposes this circuit disposes of the need of discrete battery for microcontroller, for this situation we needn't bother with a different power supply to control our Arduino; the ESC itself will give a managed +5V which can be utilized power our Arduino. There are numerous kinds of circuit which controls this voltage typically it will be straight guideline for as little as possible ESCs, however you can likewise discover ones with exchanging circuits.

Firmware: Every ESC has a firmware program composed into it by the fabricates. This firmware enormously decides how your ESC reacts; a portion of the prominent firmware is Traditional, Simon-K and BL-Heli. This firmware is additionally client programmable however we won't get into a lot of that in this instructional exercise.

Some common terms with BLDC and ESC's:

On the off chance that you have quite recently begun to work with BLDC engines, at that point you may have most likely gone over the terms like Braking, Soft start, Engine course low voltage reaction time as well as advance . How about we investigate what these terms mean.

Braking: Braking is the capacity of your BLDC engine to quit turning at the point when the throttle is expelled. This capacity is significant for multi-copters since they have to change their RPM all the more frequently to move noticeable all around.

Delicate Start: Soft start is a significant element to think about when your BLDC engine is related with apparatus. At the point when an engine has delicate beginning empowered, it won't begin pivoting quick out of the blue, it will in every case slowly increment the speed regardless of how rapidly the throttle was given. This will help us in diminishing the mileage of riggings appended with the engines (assuming any).

Engine Direction: The engine course in BLDC engines are regularly not changed during activity. However, when gathering, the client may need to alter the course in which the engine is turning. The most effortless approach to alter the course of the engine is by essentially entomb changing any two wires of the engine.

Low Voltage Stop: Once adjusted we would consistently require our BLDC engines keep running at a similar specific speed for a specific estimation of throttle. Be that as it may, this is difficult to accomplish in light of the fact that the engines will in general diminish their speed for a similar estimation of throttle as the battery voltage diminishes. To keep away from this we typically program the ESC to quit working when the battery voltage has come to underneath the limit esteem this capacity is called Low Voltage Stop and is helpful in automatons.

Reaction time: The capacity of the engine to rapidly change its speed dependent on the adjustment in throttle is called reaction time. The lesser the reaction time is the better the control will be.

Advance: Advance is an issue or progressively like a bug with BLDC engines. All BLDC engines have a smidgen of development in them. That is the point at which the stator curls are empowered the rotor is pulled in towards it on account of the perpetual magnet present on them. In the wake of getting pulled in the rotor will in general push more ahead in that equivalent bearing before the curl de-stimulates and afterward next loop empowers. This development is designated "Advance" and it will make issues like jittering, warming up, making commotion and so forth. So this is something a decent ESC should avoid without anyone else.

Alright, enough hypothesis presently let us begin with the equipment by interfacing the engine with the Arduino.

Arduino BLDC Motor Control Circuit Diagram

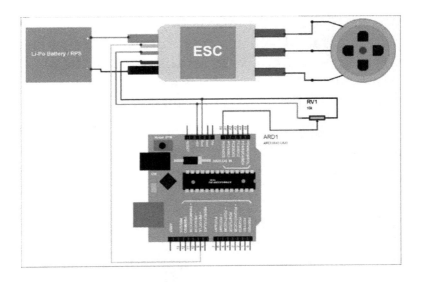

The association for interfacing BLDC engine with Arduino is really straight forward. The ESC needs a forces wellspring of around 12V as well as 5A least. In this instructional exercise I have utilized my RPS as a power source however you can likewise utilize a Li-Po battery to control the ESC. The three stage wires of the ESC ought to be associated with the three stage wires of the engines, there is no structure to interface these wires you can interface them in any request.

Cautioning: Some ESC won't have connectors on them, all things considered ensure your association is strong and secure the uncovered wires utilizing protection tape. Since there will be high current going through the stages any short would prompt lasting harm of the ESC and engine.

The BEC (Battery Eliminator circuit) in the ESC itself will direct a + 5V which can be utilized to catalyst the Arduino Board. At last to set the speed of the BLDC engine we additionally utilize a potentiometer associated with A0 stick of the Arduino

Arduino Program for BLDC Motor

We need to make a PWM signal with shifting obligation cycle from 0% to 100% with a recurrence of 50Hz. The obligation cycle ought to be constrained by utilizing a potentiometer with the goal that we can control the speed of the engine. The code to do this is like controlling the servo engines since they likewise require a PWM signal with 50Hz recurrence; consequently we utilize a similar servo library from Arduino. The total code can be found at the base of this page further underneath I clarify the code in little pieces. Furthermore, on the off chance that you are new to Arduino or PWM, at that point, first experience utilizing PWM with Arduino and controlling servo utilizing Arduino.

The PWM sign can be produced uniquely on the pins which backing PWM by equipment, these pins are ordinarily referenced with a ~ image. On Arduino UNO, the stick 9 can create PWM signal so we interface the ESC sign stick (orange wire) to stick 9 we additionally notice a similar hotel code by utilizing the accompanying line

```
ESC.attach(9);
```

We need to produce PWM sign of changing obligation

cycle from 0% to 100%. For 0% obligation cycle the POT will yield 0V (0) and for 100% obligation cycle the POT will yield 5V (1023). Here the pot is associated with stick A0, so we need to peruse the simple voltage from the POT by utilizing the simple read work as demonstrated as follows

```
int throttle = analogRead(A0);
```

At that point we need to change over the incentive from 0 to 1023 to 0 to 180 in light of the fact that the worth 0 will create 0% PWM and worth 180 will produce 100% obligation cycle. Any qualities over 180 will have neither rhyme nor reason. So we map the incentive to 0-180 by utilizing the guide work as demonstrated as follows.

```
throttle = map(throttle, 0, 1023, 0, 180);
```

At long last, we need to send this incentive to the servo capacity so it can produce the PWM signal on that stick. Since we have named out servo item as ESC the code will resemble this underneath, where the variable throttle contains the incentive from 0-180 to control the obligation cycle of the PWM signal

```
ESC.write(throttle);
```

Controlling BLDC Motor with Arduino

Make the associations as indicated by the circuit graph and transfer the code to Arduino and catalyst the ESC. Ensure you have mounted the BLDC engine onto something since the engine will hop all around while turning. When the arrangement is fueled on, your ESC will make an appreciated tone and will continue blaring until the throttle sign is inside as far as possible, straightforward increment the POT from 0V continuously and the signaling tone will stop, this implies we are presently giving PWM signal over the lower limit esteem and as you increment further your motor will start pivoting gradually. The more voltage you give the more speed the engine will get, at long last when the voltage comes to over the upper edge limit the engine will stop. You would then be able to rehash the procedure.

In the event that you had confronted any issue on getting this to work don't hesitate to utilize the remark area or utilize the gatherings for increasingly specialized assistance.

Code

```
#include <Servo.h> //Use the Servo librarey for generating PWM
Servo ESC; //name the servo object, here ESC
void setup()
{
ESC.attach(9); //Generate PWM in pin 9 of Arduino
}
void loop()
{
```

```
int throttle = analogRead(A0); //Read the voltage
from POT
throttle = map(throttle, 0, 1023, 0, 180); //Map the
values of 0-102 from pot to 0-180 bcs servo works
only from 0-180
ESC.write(throttle); //based on the value of throttle
generate PWM signal
}
```

9.DIY ARDUINO RELAY DRIVER SHIELD

In this DIY venture we make a 3-Channel Arduino Transfer Shield Circuit for transfer based applications. We structured a separated PCB for 3 transfers. By utilizing this Arduino Relay Shield, we can work 3 AC apparatuses at once. We have put a two stick screw terminal squares (Neutral, NO) for interfacing machines. Here we have given PCB format, circuit outline, and Gerber documents so you can construct or legitimately request this Relay Driver Module.

Beforehand we have fabricated 4-channel Relay Driver Module, yet this time we are building this transfer module as Arduino Shield, with the goal that you simply need to fix it over Arduino and it will be prepared to utilize. Transfers are helpful for activating home AC machines with low sign and they are utilized in Home Automation Systems.

Components Required:

- ✓ SPDT relay 12v -3
- ✓ 817 Optocoupler -3
- ✓ Transistor BC547 -3
- ✓ SMD LEDs -4
- ✓ PCB (ordered from JLCPCB) -1
- ✓ Terminal Block 2 pin -4
- ✓ 1N4007 Diode -3
- ✓ 1k Resistor -7
- ✓ Burg sticks male -1
- ✓ Jumper – 1
- ✓ Push Button
- ✓ Power supply
- ✓ Arduino for demonstration
- ✓ Connecting wire
- ✓ AC appliances

Arduino Relay Driver Shield Circuit Diagram:

Anbazhagan k

In this 3-Channel Transfer Driver Circuit, we have utilized an optocoupler to trigger the NPN transistor which further drives the hand-off. What's more, optocoupler will be activated by the dynamic LOW signal. Here we have utilized a 12v 10Amp hand-off in this PCB board, you can likewise utilize 5v transfers.

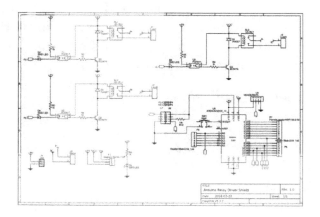

Working and Demonstration:

For exhibiting this Arduino Transfer Driver Shield, we have utilized an Arduino Uno board for controlling transfers. We have associated each of the 3 transfers with Arduino at 7, 9, and 12 pins (RLY1, RLY2, and RLY3). We have utilized a 12v connector for fueling the circuit. At that point we have associated 220VAC bulbs at the terminal square of the PCB board and AC supply is likewise connected to the board.

Complete Arduino code is given toward the part of the arrangement, code is straightforward and effectively reasonable. In the event that you need to get familiar with Relay and its interfacing with Arduino then pursue this connection.

You simply need to fix the Arduino shield over Arduino as well as control 3 machines utilizing this shield. You can utilize the given code (at last) or utilize your very own code for controlling the AC appliaces.

Circuit and PCB Design using EasyEDA:

To structure this Arduino Relay Shield, we have picked the online EDA apparatus called EasyEDA. I have recently utilized EasyEDA commonly and thought that it was advantageous to use since it has a decent accumulation of impressions and it is opensource. In the wake of planning the PCB, we can arrange the PCB tests by their ease . They additionally offer segment sourcing administration where they have a huge supply of electronic parts and clients can arrange their required segments alongside the PCB request.

While structuring your circuits and PCBs, you can likewise make your circuit and PCB plans open with the goal that different clients can duplicate or alter them and can take profit by your work, we have additionally made our entire Circuit and PCB formats open for this circuit, check the underneath connection:

You can see any Layer (Top, Base, Topsilk, bottomsilk and so on) of the PCB by choosing the layer structure the 'Layers' Window. You can likewise see the PCB, how it will care for manufacture utilizing the Photo View catch in EasyEDA:

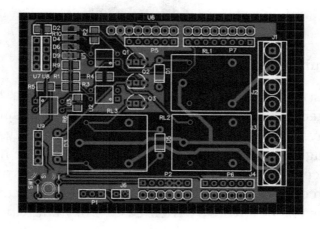

Calculating and Ordering Samples online:

Subsequent to finishing the structure of this Arduino Relay Shield, you can arrange the PCB through . To arrange the PCB from JLCPCB, you need Gerber File. To download Gerber records of your PCB simply click the Fabrication Output catch in EasyEDA editorial manager page, at that point download from the EasyEDA PCB request page.

Presently go to and click on Quote Now or Buy Now catch, at that point you can choose the quantity of PCBs you need to arrange, what number of copper layers you need, the PCB thickness, copper weight, and even the PCB shading, similar to the preview demonstrated as follows:

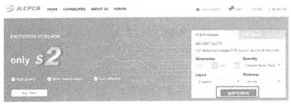

After you have chosen the majority of the choices, click "Spare to Cart" and afterward you will be taken to the page where you can transfer your Gerber File which we have downloaded from EasyEDA. Transfer your Gerber document and snap "Spare to Cart". Lastly click on Checkout Securely to finish your request, at that point you will get your PCBs a couple of days after the fact. They are creating the PCB at extremely low rate which is $2. Their manufacture time is additionally extremely less which is 48 hours with DHL conveyance of 3-5 days, essentially you will get your PCBs inside seven days of requesting.

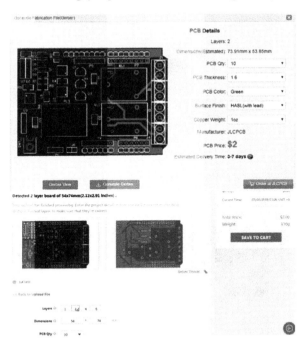

In the wake of requesting the PCB, you can check the Production Progress of your PCB with date and time. You check it by going on Account page and snap on "Generation Progress" interface under the PCB like, appeared in beneath picture.

Anbazhagan k

Following couple of long periods of requesting PCB's I got the PCB tests in decent bundling as appeared in underneath pictures.

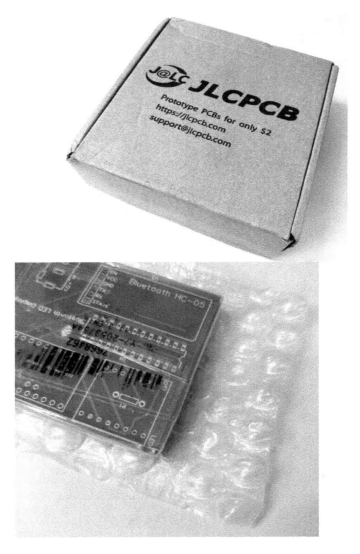

Subsequent to getting these pieces I have mounted all the required segments over the PCB associated it with

Arduino for showing.

So our Arduino Relay Shield is prepared, and you can straightforwardly utilize it with Arduino to control three AC apparatuses. You simply need to put this Arduino shield over Arduino and transfer the beneath given code. You can alter the code as per you.

Code

```
#define RLY1 7
#define RLY2 9
```

```
#define RLY3 12
void setup()
{
 pinMode(RLY1, OUTPUT);
 pinMode(RLY2, OUTPUT);
 pinMode(RLY3, OUTPUT);
 digitalWrite(RLY1, LOW);
 digitalWrite(RLY2, LOW);
 digitalWrite(RLY3, LOW);
}
void loop()
{
 digitalWrite(RLY1, HIGH);
 digitalWrite(RLY2, HIGH);
 digitalWrite(RLY3, LOW);
 delay(1000);
     digitalWrite(RLY1, HIGH);
 digitalWrite(RLY2, LOW);
 digitalWrite(RLY3, HIGH);
 delay(1000);
     digitalWrite(RLY1, LOW);
 digitalWrite(RLY2, HIGH);
 digitalWrite(RLY3, HIGH);
 delay(1000);
}
```

10.ARDUINO BASED PIANO WITH RECORDING AND REPLAY

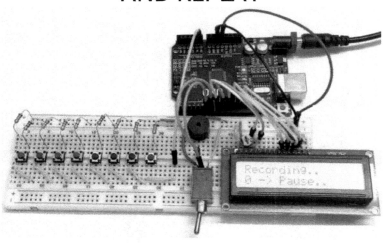

Arduino has been an aid for individuals who are not from the hardware foundation to fabricate stuff effectively. It has been an incredible prototyping apparatus or to take a stab at something cool, in this venture we are going to fabricate a little yet fun Piano utilizing the Arduino. This piano is basically plain with only 8 push catches and bell. It utilizes the tone() capacity of Arduino to make different kinds of piano notes on the speaker. To flavor it up a piece we have included the account highlight in the task, this empowers us to play a tune record it and play it again more than once when required. Sound intriguing right!! So we should get building....

Materials Required:

- ❖ Arduino Uno
- ❖ 16*2 LCD Display
- ❖ Buzzer
- ❖ Trimmer 10k
- ❖ SPDT switch
- ❖ Push button (8 Nos)
- ❖ Resistors (10k, 560R, 1.5k, 2.6k, 3.9, 5.6k, 6.8k, 8.2k, 10k)
- ❖ Breadboard
- ❖ Connecting wires

Circuit Diagram:

The total Arduino Piano Project can be based over a breadboard with some interfacing wires. The circuit outline made utilizing fritzing that demonstrates the breadboard perspective on the undertaking is demonstrated as follows

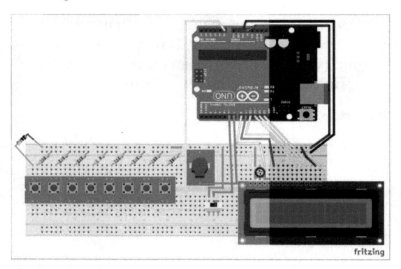

Simply pursue the circuit chart and associate the wires likewise, the push catches and signal as utilized with a PCB module however in real equipment we have utilized just the switch and bell, it ought not befuddle you much since they have a similar sort of stick out. You can likewise allude to the underneath picture of the equipment to make your associations.

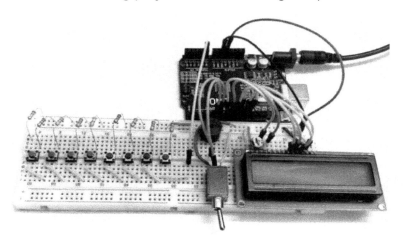

The estimation of the resistors from the left is in the accompanying request, 10k, 560R, 1.5k, 2.6k, 3.9, 5.6k, 6.8k, 8.2k and 10k. On the off chance that you don't have the equivalent DPST switch you can utilize typical flip switch like the one appeared in the circuit graph above. Presently we should investigate the schematics of the venture to comprehend why we have made the accompanying associations.

Schematics and Explanation:

The schematics for the circuit graph that is appeared above is given underneath, it was likewise made utilizing Fritzing.

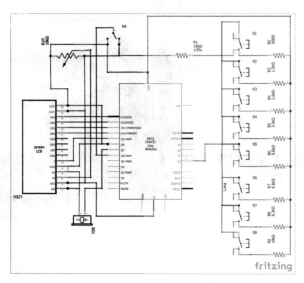

One primary association that we need to comprehend is that how we have associated the 8 push catches to the Arduino through the Analog A0 stick. Fundamentally we need 8 information pins which can be associated with the 8 information push catches, yet for tasks like this we can't utilize 8 pins of the microcontroller only for push catches since we may require them for later use. For our situation we have the LCD show to be interfaced.

So we utilize the simple stick of the Arduino and structure a potential divider with shifting resistor esteems to finish the circuit. Along these lines when each catch is squeezed an alternate simple voltage will be provided to the Analog stick. An example circuit with just two resistors and two push catches are demonstrated as follows.

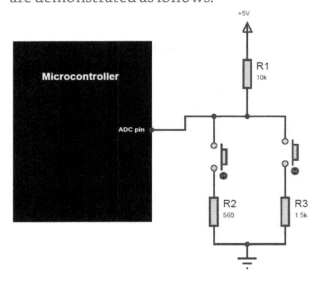

For this situation the ADC stick will get +5V when the push catches are not squeezed, on the off chance that the principal catch is squeezed, at that point the potential divider gets finished through the 560R resistor and in the event that the subsequent catch is squeezed, at that point the potential divider gets contended utilizing the 1.5k resistor. Along these lines the voltage gotten by the ADC stick will change dependent on the formulae of potential divider. On the off chance that you need to find out about how the potential divider functions and how to ascertain the estimation of voltage gotten by the ADC stick then you can utilize this potential divider adding machine page.

Other than this every one of the associations are straight forward, the LCD is associated with pins 8, 9, 10, 11 and 12. The bell is associated with the stick 7 and the SPDT switch is associated with the stick 6 of Arduino. The total venture is controlled through the USB port of the workstation. You can likewise associate the Arduino to a 9V or 12V stock through the DC jack and the venture will at present work the equivalent.

Understanding the *Tone()* function of Arduino:

The Arduino has a convenient tone() work which can be utilized to create shifting recurrence flag that can be utilized to deliver various sounds utilizing a signal. So we should see how the capacity functions and how it very well may be utilized with Arduino.

Before that we should know how a Piezo signal functions. We may have found out about Piezo precious stones in our school, it is only a gem which changes over mechanical vibrations into power or the other way around. Here we apply a variable current (recurrence) for which the precious stone vibrates in this manner creating sound. Subsequently so as to make the Piezo signal to make some clamor we need to make the Piezo electric gem to vibrate, the pitch and tone of commotion relies upon how quick the precious stone vibrates. Henceforth the tone and pitch can be constrained by shifting the recurrence of the current.

Alright, so how would we get a variable recurrence from Arduino? This is the place the tone () capacity comes in. The tone () can create a specific recurrence on a particular stick. The time length can likewise be referenced whenever required. The grammar for tone () is

Syntax

tone(pin, frequency)

tone(pin, frequency, duration)

Parameters

pin: the pin on which to generate the tone

frequency: the frequency of the tone in hertz – unsigned int

duration: the duration of the tone in milliseconds (optional 1) – unsigned long

The estimations of stick can be any of your computerized stick. I have utilized stick number 8 here. The recurrence that can be produced relies upon the size of the clock in your Arduino load up. For UNO and most other normal sheets the base recurrence that can be delivered is 31Hz and the greatest recurrence that can be created is 65535Hz. Anyway we people can hear just frequencies somewhere in the range of 2000Hz and 5000 Hz.

Playing piano tones on Arduino:

Alright, before even I begin on this point let me clarify that I am a learner with melodic notes or piano, so please excuse me on the off chance that anything referenced under this heading is rubbish.

We presently realize that we can utilize the tones work in Arduino to create a few sounds, however how might we play tones of a specific note utilizing the equivalent. Fortunate for us there is a library called "pitches.h" composed by Brett Hagman. This library contains all the data about which recurrence is proportionate to which note on a piano. I was astonished by how well this library could really function and play pretty much every note on a piano, I utilized the equivalent to play the piano notes of Pirates of Caribbean, Crazy Frog, Mario and even titanic and they sounded great. Oh no! We are getting somewhat off point here, so in the event that you are keen on that look at playing songs utilizing Arduino venture. You will likewise discover more clarification about the pitches.h library in that venture.

Our venture has just 8 push catches so each catch can play just a single specific melodic note and hence absolutely we can play just 8 notes. I chose the most utilized notes on a piano, however would you be able to can choose any 8 or even extend the venture with more push catches and include more notes.

The notes chose in this venture are the notes C4, D4, E4, F4, G4, A4, B4 and C5 which can be played utilizing the catches 1 to 8 separately.

Programming the Arduino:

Enough of hypothesis let us get to the fun piece of programming the Arduino. The total Arduino Program is given toward the part of the bargain you can bounce down in the event that you excited or read further to see how the code functions.

In our Arduino program we need to peruse the simple voltage from stick A0, at that point anticipate which catch was squeezed and play the individual tone for that catch. While doing this we ought to likewise record which catch the client has squeezed and to what extent he/she has squeezed, so we can reproduce the tone that was played by the client later.

Before heading off to the rationale part, we need to pronounce which 8 notes we will play. The particular recurrence for the notes is then taken from the pitches.h library and after that a cluster is framed as demonstrated as follows. Here the recurrence to play note C4 is 262, etc.

```
int notes[] = {262, 294, 330, 349, 392, 440, 494,
523}; // Set frequency for C4, D4, E4, F4, G4, A4, B4,
```

Next we need to referenced to which sticks the LCD show is associated with. In case you are following precisely the same schematics given above, at that point you don't need to transform anything here.

```
const int rs = 8, en = 9, d4 = 10, d5 = 11, d6 = 12, d7 =
13; //Pins to which LCD is connected

LiquidCrystal lcd(rs, en, d4, d5, d6, d7);
```

Next, inside our arrangement work we simply introduce the LCD module and sequential screen for investigating. We additionally show an introduction message just to ensure things are functioning as arranged. Next, inside the fundamental circle work we have two while circles.

One while circle will be executed as long as the SPDT switch is put in account more. In account mode the client can pay the tones required and simultaneously the tone that is being played will likewise be spared. So the while circle resembles this beneath

```
while (digitalRead(6) == 0) //If the toggle switch
is set in recording mode

{

    lcd.setCursor(0, 0); lcd.print("Recording..");

    lcd.setCursor(0, 1);

    Detect_button();

    Play_tone();

}
```

As you may have seen we have two capacities inside the while circle. The principal work Detect_button() is utilized discover which catch the client has squeezed and the second work Play_tone() is utilized to play the particular tone. Aside from this capacity the Detect_button() work likewise records which catch is being squeezed and the Play_tone() work records to what extent the catch was squeezed.

Inside the Detect_button() work we read the simple voltage from the stick A0 and contrast it with some predefined values with discover which catch has been squeezed. The worth can be dictated by either utilizing the voltage divider adding machine above or by utilizing the sequential screen to check what simple worth is perused for each catch.

```
void Detect_button()

{

  analogVal = analogRead(A0); //read the analog
voltag on pin A0

  pev_button = button; //remember the previous
button pressed by the user

  if (analogVal < 550)

    button = 8;

  if (analogVal < 500)

    button = 7;

  if (analogVal < 450)

    button = 6;

  if (analogVal < 400)

    button = 5;

  if (analogVal < 300)
```

```
button = 4;

if (analogVal < 250)

button = 3;

if (analogVal < 150)

button = 2;

if (analogVal < 100)

button = 1;

if (analogVal > 1000)

button = 0;

/****Rcord the pressed buttons in a array***/

if (button != pev_button && pev_button != 0)

{

recorded_button[button_index] = pev_button;

button_index++;

recorded_button[button_index] = 0;
```

```
    button_index++;

  }

  /**End of Recording program**/

  }
```

As stated, inside this capacity we additionally record the arrangement where the catches are squeezed. The recorded qualities are put away in an exhibit named recorded_button[]. We first check in case there is another catch squeezed, whenever squeezed then we likewise check in case it isn't the catch 0. Where catch 0 is only no catch is squeezed. Inside the if circle we store the incentive on the list area given by the variable button_index and after that we likewise increment this list esteem with the goal that we don't over compose on a similar area.

```
  /****Rcord the pressed buttons in a array***/

  if (button != pev_button && pev_button != 0)

  {

    recorded_button[button_index] = pev_button;

    button_index++;
```

```
    recorded_button[button_index] = 0;

    button_index++;

}
```

/End of Recording program**/**

Inside the Play_tone() work we will play the separate tone for the catch squeezed by utilizing numerous if conditions. Likewise we will utilize an exhibit named recorded_time[] inside which we will spare the time span for which the catch was squeezed. The activity is like chronicle catch grouping by we utilize the millis() capacity to decide to what extent each catch was squeezed, additionally for decreasing the size of the variable we isolate the incentive by 10. For catch 0, which means the client isn't squeezing anything we play no tone for a similar length. The total code inside the capacity is demonstrated as follows.

```
void Play_tone()

{

/****Rcord the time delay between each button press in a array***/

    if (button != pev_button)
```

```
{

   lcd.clear(); //Then clean it

   note_time = (millis() - start_time) / 10;

   recorded_time[time_index] = note_time;

   time_index++;

   start_time = millis();

}

/**End of Recording program**/

if (button == 0)

{

   noTone(7);

   lcd.print("0 -> Pause..");

}

if (button == 1)

{
```

```
    tone(7, notes[0]);

  lcd.print("1 -> NOTE_C4");

}

if (button == 2)

{

  tone(7, notes[1]);

  lcd.print("2 -> NOTE_D4");

}

if (button == 3)

{

  tone(7, notes[2]);

  lcd.print("3 -> NOTE_E4");

}

if (button == 4)

{
```

```
  tone(7, notes[3]);

  lcd.print("4 -> NOTE_F4");

}

if (button == 5)

{

  tone(7, notes[4]);

  lcd.print("5 -> NOTE_G4");

}

if (button == 6)

{

  tone(7, notes[5]);

  lcd.print("6 -> NOTE_A4");

}

if (button == 7)

{
```

```
    tone(7, notes[6]);

    lcd.print("7 -> NOTE_B4");

  }

  if (button == 8)

  {

    tone(7, notes[7]);

    lcd.print("8 -> NOTE_C5");

  }

}
```

At last in the wake of account the client needs to flip the DPST to the next heading to play the recorded tone. At the point when this is done the program breaks out of the past while circle and enters the second while circle where we play the notes in the grouping of the catches squeezed for a span that was recently recorded. The code to do the equivalent is demonstrated as follows.

```
while (digitalRead(6) == 1) //If the toggle switch
is set in Playing mode
```

```
{

lcd.clear();

lcd.setCursor(0, 0); lcd.print("Now Playing..");

for (int i = 0; i < sizeof(recorded_button) / 2; i++)

{

delay((recorded_time[i]) * 10); //Wait for before
paying next tune

if (recorded_button[i] == 0)

noTone(7); //user dint touch any button

else

tone(7, notes[(recorded_button[i] - 1)]); //play
the sound corresponding to the button touched by
the user

}

}

}
```

Play, Record, Replay and Repeat! :

Make the equipment according to the circuit outline appeared, and transfer the code to the Arduino load up and its demonstrated time. Position the SPDT in the chronicle mode and start playing your preferred tones, squeezing each catch will deliver an alternate tone. During this mode the LCD will show "Recording..." and on the second line you will see the name of the note that is right now being squeezed as demonstrated as follows

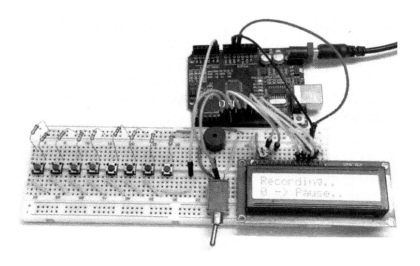

When you have played your tone flip the SPDT change to the opposite side and the LCD should show "Now Playing.." and afterward start playing the tone that you simply played. A similar tone will be played over and over as long as the flip switch is kept in the situation as appeared in the beneath picture.

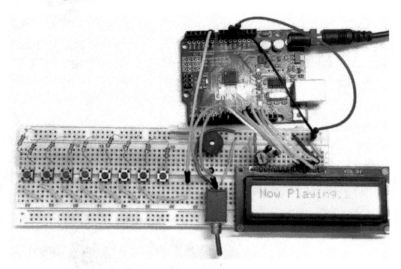

Expectation you comprehended the task and delighted in structure it.

Code

```
/*

  Arduino based Piano and Record and play option

*/
#include <LiquidCrystal.h>
int notes[] = {262, 294, 330, 349, 392, 440, 494,
523}; // Set frequency for C4, D4, E4, F4, G4, A4, B4, C5
const int rs = 8, en = 9, d4 = 10, d5 = 11, d6 = 12, d7 =
13; //Pins to which LCD is connected
LiquidCrystal lcd(rs, en, d4, d5, d6, d7);
char button = 0;
int analogVal;
```

```
char REC = 0;
int recorded_button[200];
int pev_button;
int recorded_time [200];
char time_index;
char button_index = 0;
unsigned long start_time;
int note_time;
void setup() {
  Serial.begin(9600);
 pinMode (6, INPUT);
  lcd.begin(16, 2); //We are using a 16*2 LCD display
 lcd.print("Arduino Piano"); //Display a intro message
  lcd.setCursor(0, 1);   // set the cursor to column 0,
line 1
  lcd.print("-Hello"); //Display a intro message
  delay(2000); //Wait for display to show info
  lcd.clear(); //Then clean it
}
void loop()
{
  while (digitalRead(6) == 0) //If the toggle switch is
set in recording mode
  {
  lcd.setCursor(0, 0); lcd.print("Recording..");
  lcd.setCursor(0, 1);
    Detect_button();
  Play_tone();
  }
```

```
  while (digitalRead(6) == 1) //If the toggle switch is
set in Playing mode
{
lcd.clear();
lcd.setCursor(0, 0); lcd.print("Now Playing..");
  for (int i = 0; i < sizeof(recorded_button) / 2; i++)
{
  delay((recorded_time[i]) * 10); //Wait for before pay-
ing next tune
    if (recorded_button[i] == 0)
    noTone(7); //user dint touch any button
    else
      tone(7, notes[(recorded_button[i] - 1)]); //play the
sound corresponding to the button touched by the
user
}
}
}
void Detect_button()
{
 analogVal = analogRead(A0); //read the analog voltag
on pin A0
 pev_button = button; //remember the previous
button pressed by the user
  if (analogVal < 550)
  button = 8;
  if (analogVal < 500)
  button = 7;
```

```
if(analogVal < 450)
button = 6;
if(analogVal < 400)
button = 5;
if(analogVal < 300)
button = 4;
if(analogVal < 250)
button = 3;
if(analogVal < 150)
button = 2;
if(analogVal < 100)
button = 1;
if(analogVal > 1000)
button = 0;


/****Rcord the pressed buttons in a array***/
if(button != pev_button && pev_button != 0)
{
  recorded_button[button_index] = pev_button;
  button_index++;
  recorded_button[button_index] = 0;
  button_index++;
}
/**End of Recording program**/
}
void Play_tone()
{
  /****Rcord the time delay between each button press
```

```
in a array***/
 if (button != pev_button)
 {
  lcd.clear(); //Then clean it
  note_time = (millis() - start_time) / 10;
    recorded_time[time_index] = note_time;
  time_index++;
    start_time = millis();
}
/**End of Recording program**/
 if (button == 0)
 {
 noTone(7);
 lcd.print("0 -> Pause..");
 }

 if (button == 1)
 {
 tone(7, notes[0]);
 lcd.print("1 -> NOTE_C4");
 }

 if (button == 2)
 {
 tone(7, notes[1]);
 lcd.print("2 -> NOTE_D4");
 }

 if (button == 3)
 {
 tone(7, notes[2]);
 lcd.print("3 -> NOTE_E4");
 }
```

```
if (button == 4)
{
tone(7, notes[3]);
lcd.print("4 -> NOTE_F4");
}
if (button == 5)
{
tone(7, notes[4]);
lcd.print("5 -> NOTE_G4");
}
if (button == 6)
{
tone(7, notes[5]);
lcd.print("6 -> NOTE_A4");
}
if (button == 7)
{
tone(7, notes[6]);
lcd.print("7 -> NOTE_B4");
}
if (button == 8)
{
tone(7, notes[7]);
lcd.print("8 -> NOTE_C5");
}
}
```

www.ingramcontent.com/pod-product-compliance
Lightning Source LLC
Chambersburg PA
CBHW071128050326
40690CB00008B/1375